About

One Drop Awareness:
Picturing Enlightenment and Nonduality

"This isn't a short book, but it is a friendly one. It's got jokes, po-ems, quotes, creative typesetting, and illustrations. It's got ma-ture humility, generosity and a grace of expression that make it a pleasure to read. Besides the light-hearted tone, what I like best is that Tom brings his rich background into play. Tantra, dream work, healing and indigenous traditions are treated as helpful, and not as exceptions to nondual teaching. I must say that this book makes me want to know the author better."

Greg Goode, author of *Standing as Awareness*

"I've often thought that we haven't yet touched upon the power of the visual to point to the freedom known as nonduality. With *One Drop Awareness*, Tom Crockett has taken a pioneering step in that direction. This is a simple, easy-to-read, interesting and intelligent book. It's the kind of pointing that can reach anyone because it peels the message down to really basic images and pointers without stripping it of its beauty. Simplicity is always good, especially with something as ineffable as nonduality. I rec-ommend this!"

Scott Kiloby, author of *Reflections of the One Life*
and *Living Realization*

"Awakening, holistic awareness and enlightenment are common themes in spiritual literature, but are just as commonly misunderstood. *One Drop Awareness* is a delightful introductory book that utilizes illustrations, metaphors and clear language to demystify the mystical."

Master Charles Cannon, author of *The Bliss of Freedom* and Spiritual Director of Synchronicity Foundation for Modern Spirituality

"Oh my, I am so deeply moved and grateful to have read this book. Several times throughout the book, I found myself crying, each tear a drop of recognition. *One Drop Awareness* has nailed some of our deepest questions and shown both visually and with clear, simple language, the truth of who we are and what our lives can be if we open to that 'one drop' of awareness. Tom Crockett has aptly demonstrated that the human experience is both so intimate and so universal. I felt I was reading a diary of my own soul. The question "What does it all boil down to?" can be answered here in 'One Drop.'"

Kia Scherr, founder of *One Life Alliance*

"Thank God for the creative vision of artists when unfolding the apparent mystery of nonduality. The ineffable seems better served by the gentle hands of the artist. Though both speak to the same wisdom, I find the poetry of Rumi endlessly more nourishing than the picture perfect presentation of the same food by Wei Wu Wei.

So be it with Tom Crockett and *One Drop Awareness*. I welcome this simple, direct and instantaneous method of nondual expression which freely paints with the extended palette of metaphoric imagery, humor and poetic expression. For those interested in the expression of our innate freedom as awareness through art and entertainment, this book is a refreshing attempt to point at the love that permeates this majestic celebration, setting melodic, gentle alarms designed to awaken us from this slumber of perceived containment.

As Crockett says, this book of textual and visual nudges "plays passionately with words and images," a playful primer, almost winking at the reader, ever reminding him that the picture of food is not food itself. The dangers of the task are not lost on him. *One Drop Awareness* is an attempt to reveal what thoughts, feelings and perceptions point to: the ineffable and its tangible perfume as Truth, Love and Beauty.

There is a joy in this book, fueled by a natural curiosity that just may tickle you in ways far more subtle than other books, It is a passionate engagement and the fingerprints of awakening peak out from it: compassion, love and playfulness permeate it. Kudos for Crockett's attempt to take Nonduality out of the closet of concept and into the living room of experience in an accessible and creative way."

Chris Hebard, creator of *StillnessSpeaks.com*

ONE DROP
AWARENESS

PICTURING ENLIGHTENMENT
AND NONDUALITY

*Terri,
Thanks for Integral Life Practice.*

Tom Crockett

BLISS PRESS

Newport News, Virginia

Published in 2011 by
Bliss Press
2 Indian Springs Drive
Newport News, VA 23606

ISBN-13: 978-1460940679
ISBN-10: 1460940679

Cover and Book Design by Tom Crockett

Acknowledgments

I have been very lucky to have a spiritual community that has allowed me to incubate and gestate these ideas in thousands of hours of online and personal satsang. I have deep gratitude for Susan, Siglia, Leilani, Zannie, Greg, Paul, Nisha, Jasmine, Paula, Diana, Lucanne, Premshanti, Linda, Stan, Jude, Deborah, Margaret, Crystal, Riesah, Patricia, and Steve. They have asked deep and penetrating questions and this book might not have come into being if not for them.

I am also grateful for the friendship and intellectual stimulation of Carl Hyatt. Again, there is a direct link between this book and his support. The greatest teachers I have had in the art of appreciating each moment as it arises have been the children I have been lucky enough to watch grow and evolve into amazing beings: Holly, Kasey, and Dylan. Finally, I am blessed to be reminded everyday that if I can find oneness with one other being, as I do with my wife and beloved, Kelly Leigh, then it must be true—I must be one with everything.

CONTENTS

Mantra For A Writer

Because certainty is an occupational hazard
for those who commit words to pages.

I don't know anything. I don't know anything. I don't know
anything. I don't know anything. I don't know anything. I
don't know anything. I don't know anything. I don't know
anything. I don't know anything. I don't know anything. I
don't know anything. I don't know anything. I don't know
anything. I don't know anything. I don't know anything. I
don't know anything. I don't know anything. I don't know
anything. I don't know anything. I don't know anything. I
don't know anything. I don't know anything. I don't know
anything. I don't know anything. I don't know anything. I
don't know anything. I don't know anything. I don't know
anything. I don't know anything. I don't know anything. I
don't know anything. I don't know anything. I don't know
anything. I don't know anything. I don't know anything. I
don't know anything. I don't know anything. I don't know
anything. I don't know anything. I don't know anything. I
don't know anything. I don't know anything. I don't know
anything. I don't know anything. I don't know anything. I
don't know anything. I don't know anything. I don't know
anything. **Okay, so I have these occasional ideas. But I don't
really know anything.** I don't know anything. I don't know
anything. I don't know anything. I don't know anything. I

ONE DROP

I am.
I am nothing.
I am nothing like a still dark pool.
I am nothing like a still dark pool
in a perfect obsidian cave.
Me looking at me for millennia.
I am nothing like a still dark pool.
I am nothing.

And yet, when a perfect liquid tear,
a pebble-sized piece of me,
drops from somewhere and lands nowhere,
I feel a ripple of tiny waves,
a divine tremor,
that I should not feel
if I am nothing.

And so love begins.

Am I the pool or the ripples,
the hand on my lover's thigh
or the quiver as she opens?

Was there a time
I did not live in anticipation?

ENLIGHTENMENT

If we knew what enlightenment actually was,
would we really want it?

Because it isn't a self-help program.

It won't save your relationship or attract all your
worldly desires to you through some cosmic law.

It isn't the end of pain.

You will not find anything you don't already have.

It's simply the truth,
and the truth is an acquired taste.

Introduction
Something & Nothing

Some people believe that enlightenment
is a realization of absolute emptiness.
"We are all nothing (no-thing)."

Some people believe that enlightenment
is a realization of absolute oneness.
"We are all one (the same thing)."

What interests me is what is the relationship of
something to nothing.

The first thing you need to know is that no matter how much spiritual practice you have done or will do, at the end of this book or at the end of a lifetime of practicing and seeking, you will not have anything that you do not already have right here, right now.

The awakened or enlightened or liberated or self-realized version of yourself is who and what you already are. When you are dreaming at night and you wake up, you are not more you or a better you than you were a few moments earlier. You are simply awake.

The GOD that is dreaming you and me and all of us is the GOD that is expressing consciousness through us. That GOD—that consciousness—does not come and go. It is always there. We simply forget that is true. We forget who we are. We are asleep and dreaming.

My vision in writing this book was to create a kind of visual and textual version of those beautiful Zen alarm clocks that waken us gradually with soft chimes, calling us back into consciousness and presence.

You can't write an appropriate introduction to a book until after you've written it for the same reason that you can't really introduce a person you do not know. This makes an introduction for a book an odd experience for the author because for the reader it is the beginning, while for the author, it is the ending.

In the case of this book, however, that is a good thing because I discovered what I was writing about as I was writing. I had this experience (or series of experiences) that haunted me, changed me, caused me to question who "me" was. I began to doubt that the "me" I had grown so comfortable with even existed. This was not an easy thing to talk about with anyone. It was, in fact, damn inconvenient.

I tried writing to better understand what was going on. I wrote as a form of direct inquiry. I wrote to see what answers would arise. I wrote to people who looked to me for some sense of clarity, always afraid that if I was honest, it would not comfort but overwhelm. Most people don't really want enlightenment. They are not unhappy enough or disillusioned enough for a game-changing, life-altering "truth" to be their first choice. And if they are suffering, there are far more attractive options (and teachers to teach them) out there that promise to alleviate suffering short of having to face the truth of existence.

I wrote this book for two reasons. First, I had a genuine question about the relationship between doing and not doing. There is a big divide between those suggesting that if we do this or do that, we will change and feel better, grow and evolve, and those who say that nothing needs to be done and that seeking anything—striving for or doing anything—is what is causing our suffering. Both things seem to be true, depending on where you are standing.

Another way of phrasing this might be, to acknowledge that there is a me that seems to:

- grow stronger and more flexible
  from practicing yoga;
- get better at playing the guitar
  by practicing the guitar;
- become healthier from eating simple living foods;
- get less attached to my own identity
  from meditating;
- function better with others
  by communicating more clearly;
- become a better runner by running;
- get more centered and grounded
  from practicing tai chi;
- express my heart better
  by reading and writing poetry;
- gain more awareness of energy
  by practicing chi gung;
- deepen my relationship with my partner

through tantric practice;
- become a better friend
by learning to listen more deeply;
- increase my sense of compassion
through prayer and service;

And there is a me that is perfect as I am in this moment, either because any sense of me or my form is an illusion—an artifact of perception in this realm—or because I am GOD— arising as a temporary wave of GOD on an ocean of GOD? As Zen Master Suzuki Roshi would explain to his students *"You're all perfect as you are, and you could use a little improvement."*

The me that engages in practice or discipline in any form seems to require some desire to grow, evolve, improve, or refine that form. While at the same time there is a me that recognizes a futility or perhaps a trap inherent in seeking anything. It seems that there is something immensely important in the recognition of the illusory nature of all form (and in referring to "all form" I include my sense of "me"). But I can also find value in the yoga of working or playing with the "me" form in this life as an artist might work with the medium of clay or light or paint on canvas.

Artist and teacher, Rupert Spira, has noted, when we recognize nonduality through the mind, we call it truth or understanding. When we recognize it through our relationship to another (whether the divine or the incarnation of the beloved), we call it love. When we recognize it through the perception of the forms the world takes, we call this beauty.

Ideas of the mind are not nonduality, but neither are the relationships of the heart, nor the art or artifacts of perception. They can, however, point us toward a nondual awareness, which brings me to the second purpose of this book.

I wrote this book as an exploration and a collection of visual and textual pointing out instructions—nudges in the direction of enlightenment.

Several years ago, in an especially intense period of prayer, study, meditation, and fasting, I had this waking dream or vision.

At first I feel as though I am looking down from the center of the ceiling of an obsidian dome cave. I feel this more than see this, because there is nothing to see. I gradually become aware that I have no form. I am the cave ceiling and the still black mirror pool below, though I also know that the stuff of the cave and the stuff that makes up the pool are the same stuff. I am looking down and looking up at the same moment.

It is the most deeply peaceful feeling I have ever experienced and, in an odd way, the most frightening feeling I have ever felt. I want nothing. I need nothing. That is liberating. But I am nothing. There is no me to do, to accomplish, to act, to control my own destiny, to ensure my own happiness. That is terrifying. I am the void dreaming of the void. I am bliss dreaming of bliss. I extend infinitely backward and forward in time and am nothing but this absolute moment.

There is no source of light in this space, so I do not know how I can see, but I do see and feel a single drop of water gain weight and form and press against the domed ceiling as if stretching out for the water below. I am the ceiling and the drop and the pool that awaits the drop's return. This gesture seems to take forever.

I watch the drop of water fall away from "me" and await its falling into "me," all in a kind of beautiful slow motion. When the drop lands, I have the first sense of there being an embodied me to feel it. I feel it between my eyes, in my heart, and deep in my belly. It is the big bang and the first heartbeat.

From above I see the ripples from the drop rolling out in tiny circular waves. From within, I feel those ripples as a shiver or tremor going through my newly embodied form. Up to that moment, everything had simply been perception. After that moment, the first thought: "Everything is different now."

And then I awoke.

The best way I have of describing the lingering experience of this vision is that I felt like I had arrived at something like a truly natural state of being. I was aware of thoughts, but I wasn't thinking them. I was abiding as awareness itself, but I wasn't separate from the me of which I had awareness. I was not detached from the me that was having experiences.

Having an habitually busy mind, this was a dramatic experience for me. This was not just an altered state of consciousness, but a sort of dropping away of all states of consciousness. I have since read more about what nondual or pure awareness is or is supposed to be (there is a surprising diversity of opinion about what nonduality is) and I initially felt some sense of unworthiness. I had not spent years in deep monastic meditation or sat at the feet of a famous guru. I was not aiming at this thing called nonduality or enlightenment. I was motivated by the desire to help people with very real problems in their life and this nonduality thing only promised to make things far worse before (if ever) it made anything better. I was seeking the truth, foolishly challenging the universe with "at whatever cost." If I was doing anything, it was relentlessly asking questions about the nature of things.

I also felt a sense of unworthiness because my vision came to me as, well, a vision—imagery—and imagery is so often dismissed among teachers who write about nonduality. But, having been trained as an artist, probably made me more inclined to experience things in terms of visual or metaphoric imagery.

Having spent time as a school teacher makes me sensitive to the fact that some people learn best by reading words or hearing things explained in words (visual or auditory linguistic learners). Other people learn best by manipulating things with their hands (kinesthetic experiential learners). And some people learn best by seeing pictures (visual symbolic learners). I tend to sketch things, make little diagrams, and speak in metaphoric language, so that is the form this book has taken.

Honestly there aren't many picture books about enlightenment, pure awareness, or nonduality (*probably for good reason*), but, since I don't <u>need</u> to do anything because I am perfect as I am, and since I understand the trap in seeking my identity in the creation of some other form, I don't suppose there is any harm in playing passionately with words and images and pulling them together to form a book.

I will also apologize in advance for treating this subject with some humor and inquisitiveness. So many teachers in the nondual tradition in the West seem to be so earnest and serious about their revelations. I don't mean any disrespect. I just think that the truth of nondual awareness should liberate us to a more passionate engagement with the world.

I also understand that for some people, nondual awareness is *simply true*. It needs no other value than that it is true. For other people, however, nondual awareness is also *useful* in that it seems to bring an end to the suffering associated with separation and striving. Being something of a pragmatic mystic, I appreciate the truth, but find the usefulness, well, useful.

This is not meant to be the final word on enlightenment and nonduality. There are teachers and writers with a far greater depth of understanding than I possess. I am also writing as something of an outsider. I have been that dreaded thing—a self-confessed "spiritual seeker" and spiritual teacher—for nearly three decades and, if I have any kind of expertise, it is in knowing what doesn't work, at least what doesn't work for long.

I am not a guru. I am not even a very good teacher. I don't know that I will ever reach that point where my eyes will glaze over in rapture as I pontificate on how there is no "me" anymore, but I do identify less and less with the "me" that has been seeking and teaching for so long.

As I have written, this book is kind of a visual primer. Though I have read widely and learned a lot from other teachers, what I'm presenting in this book is expressed through a filter that I'm not sure those teachers would agree with. As much as anything, this book is a collection of the answers that have arisen from asking myself the most difficult questions about my own dissatisfactions and longing.

It is also important to stress that I'm communicating with words and pictures, but there is nothing special in the words or pictures. They are just pointers. When is comes to nondual realization, pointing out is the best we can do. I am consciousness pointing out consciousness. That doesn't make me special. That doesn't make the words special. If the words don't point you to anything useful, let them go, but if they do point you to something useful, you also have to let them go. There is nothing in the words that you need to hang on to.

The challenge in talking about something like this is that I have to use concepts to describe a radical lack of conceptualization. I will use metaphors that draw distinctions: distinctions between emptiness and form, between oceans and waves, between waking and dreaming, but they are all just teaching tools. There are not two things, only one.

This is neither a religious book nor an anti-religious book. I have been a student of indigenous healing traditions and shamanism, classical and contemporary dreamwork, the Tao and Vajrayana and Zen Buddhism, but I believe the idea of enlightenment and nonduality might be said to be beyond God or religion or even spiritual concepts. Of course it may also be true that God is just another name for that natural state—that arising.

I use the term enlightenment, pure awareness, awakening, nondual realization, and liberation pretty much interchangeably throughout the book, even though I am aware that some people may differentiate between these terms.

As a literary convention in this book, when I write the word GOD, I am simply being economical and using the least amount of letters to represent in language what is undefinable.

If GOD doesn't work for you, let it go. Please feel free to translate GOD into the word with which you most resonate.

The Divine

The Source

Oneness

Emptiness or Stillness

Spirit

Consciousness

The Universal Field

The Beloved

Big Mind/Big Heart

Ground or Space

The Absolute

Brahman

Truth or Love

Pure Awareness

Buddha Nature

A Higher Power

Taoists say that the mystery that can be explained is not the mystery, and the God that can be known is not God.

A note on organization: The flow of this book is from odd-numbered page on the right (the recto) to odd-numbered page. Consider reading each chapter completely from right page to right page first.

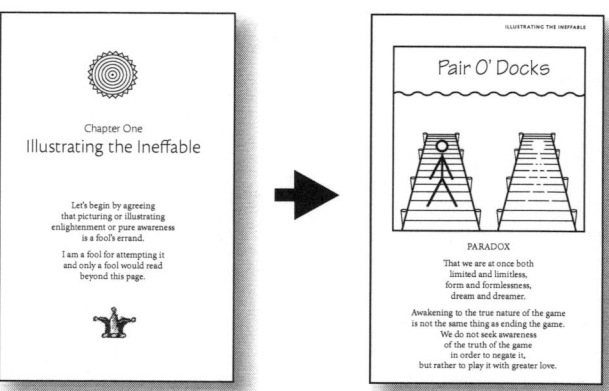

Then, if you choose, go back and work your way through the left or even-numbered pages (the verso).

The left or even-numbered page "Musings," contain text and observations that may illuminate and elaborate upon or may obfuscate and confuse the point of the facing page. Read them at your own peril.

One of my illusions is that there is a "me" that is an orderly and systematic thinker, but, this book probably shows no evidence of that. Each chapter addresses the concept of nondual awareness from a slightly different perspective. They are different ways of pointing toward something that tends to be rather illusive.

My hope is that at least one chapter or way of approaching this topic might resonate with at least one reader.

Chapter One
Illustrating the Ineffable

Let's begin by agreeing
that picturing or illustrating
enlightenment or pure awareness
is a fool's errand.

I am a fool for attempting it
and only a fool would read
beyond this page.

Musings:

 The game

Forget for the moment everything you know about American football or rugby.

What if you dreamed yourself onto a field in which you were handed an odd-shaped ball and were expected to carry it down the field and across a line, while opponents did everything in their power to stop you, including blocking you, chasing you, and painfully slamming your body to the ground? And what if the rules of this contest seemed arbitrary and capricious and the only way you discovered them was by making mistakes and being penalized? And what if there was at once an urgency about the time you had to complete this task and no end to the contest itself? Would this not feel like some outer rim of hell?

Now one level of expanded awareness might be to discover the point and purpose of the contest and to learn the rules and how to use them in your favor. This is the motivation behind the entire self-help movement and most of the contemporary spirituality movement. You might get better at the contest. You might even master it, but you are still stuck in the dream of the game.

But what if you awoke to realize that this contest was not only just a game, but a dream of a game. What if you woke to the realization that the ball and your team and your opponents and the fans and the game itself and the suffering and the elation were all you, all along. There was never anything but you.

Upon awakening from such a dream, many spiritual seekers attempt to renounce dreaming, like an addict swearing off a drug of choice. Some people, however, choose to reenter the dream with more awareness, compassion, love, and playfulness, for the sake of all beings.

PARADOX

That we are at once both
limited and limitless,
form and formlessness,
dream and dreamer.

Awakening to the true nature of the game
is not the same thing as ending the game.
We do not seek awareness
of the truth of the game
in order to negate it,
but rather to play it with greater love.

Musings:

 ## What is nonduality?

In Sanskrit there is a word "advaita" (uhd-vay-tuh). Advaita literally means "not two." It is usually translated as nondual.

There is actually no such "thing" as nonduality, because the moment you have a "thing" called nonduality, you need to have a "thing" that is duality with which to contrast it, and so you are back to two things.

Some people use the word nonduality to mean a kind of anti-duality in the same way that we might refer to matter and antimatter. This gets reinforced when we speak in metaphors that draw either/or distinctions, but nonduality actually encompasses both the matter and the antimatter—the figure and the ground. It can do that because it is not a thing at all.

Nonduality is, more accurately, an awareness, a state, a recognition that all things arise from the same ground and the appearance of difference and distinction is just that—an appearance—or a distraction, or, to use another beautiful Sanskrit word, it is Maya (illusion).

Nondualism is a strange concept for us to grasp because if we say that nondualism is a perception or experience, then we need to have a perceiver and that puts us right back in a dualistic conception. In nondual awareness, perceiver and perceived cannot be distinguished from one another. Some people get around this by speaking of a realization of oneness, but that seems to still suggest there is a realizer.

So nondualism is better described as a recognition without a recognizer. You cannot practice nondualism, but you can ask questions intended to help you realize the nondual nature of existence. This is called direct inquiry.

Because I have to start somewhere,
let's say this is GOD.

Not the square, but what is inside the square <u>and</u>
what is not inside the square, which is really not a
square, but a symbol to represent infinite space or
absolute awareness.

This is not GOD (though it actually is).

It is a picture of what GOD is and what GOD isn't
combined in nondual awareness.

There, I'm glad I cleared that up.

Musings:

 And you might ask yourself,
how do I get there?

When the expatriate writer, Gertrude Stein returned to California on a speaking tour, she was unable to find her childhood home in Oakland. Her now famous quote, "there is no there there," illuminates the first challenge with this question.

Enlightenment, awareness, or nondual realization is not a destination. There is no place to get to. We are like spiritual fish trying to find the ocean. The ocean is ever-present and always with us. It is the absolute truth and the ground of our being. We don't need to find it or discover it. We don't need to change our state. In fact, any effort expended changing a state is a distraction when it comes to realizing the true and absolute nature of reality.

What we might do is simply recognize what is already true. To this end, the "practices" of nondual awareness consist of strategies for bringing our attention to what is arising right in front of us. These strategies consist of pointing out instructions, meditations and contemplations, koans, poems, parables, and sometimes even illustrations.

There is in the literature, sometimes a suggestion that being in the presence of someone who has truly awakened is often enough to call someone into wakefulness spontaneously, but this usually seems to be one of those distracting state changes or a glimpse, rather than a stabilized awareness.

I once dreamed that Ken Wilber was smacking me in the back of the head with each of the many books he has written in an attempt to bring me to enlightenment. He kept saying "Wake up! Wake up!" until I actually woke up.

This line is GOD. It extends infinitely. It has no beginning and no

This line is also GOD.

It is pure potential.
There is nothing that is not this line.
There is no form this line cannot draw.
We are all made of the same line-stuff.
Everything is made of the same line-stuff.

Musings:

 What does awakening mean?

Quite simply, it means realizing the truth about yourself—the truth about everything. The "you" that you "think" you are is an identity (an artifice) constructed of thoughts. We might identify three aspects of that constructed self. There is the recollected self, the anticipated self, and the evaluative self.

The recollected self is the part of you that is attached to the past. If I ask you a question about yourself, you are most likely answering from the recollected self. Your name is not who you are. It is what you remember that someone once called you. All the details of your life are simply the thoughts you have about a past with which you identify. Everything you think you know about yourself is constructed from the thoughts of the recollected self.

The anticipated self is the part of you that is attached to the future. The anticipated self is always either afraid or anxious about what will or will not happen. Will I get what I want? How will this work out? Will I get hurt? Will it last?

The evaluative self is that part of you that seems to be in the present, but is consumed with evaluating experience as it arises based on preferences that reinforce a separate identity.

We come to think of our thoughts as being who we are, but this is not true. We believe we are bound by time, but time is just an appearance, a convention that supports an identity that is seldom actually present in the moment. Between our recollections and our anticipations and our judgment of what we do find arising, we live in an illusion.

Awakening or nondual realization is what happens when that constructed self dissolves, leaving only the timeless sense of awareness and presence.

end.

Of course, the moment I say "This line is GOD,"
you might quite logically ask,
"What is all of the stuff that is not the line?"

Well that's GOD too,
(that's the challenge of illustrating the ineffable).
Drawing only works because there is both
figure (line) and ground (space).
They are inseparable.

It may be that incarnation in this realm
also only works
because there is figure and ground.

Musings:

 Is nonduality a religion?

The specific religious or spiritual traditions that have explored nondual awareness most profoundly, are Advaita Vedanta from the Hindu tradition, Taoism, and the various waves of Buddhism (Theraveda, Mahayana, and Varjrayana) that emphasize, respectively, the cessation of egoic mental activity for individual enlightenment, the turn to an oceanic emptiness as a path to enlightenment for the sake of all beings, and the embrace of all forms that arise as aspects of the oneness. But, again, it is important to note that these schools of thought and practice are far from the only place in which nondual awareness can be found.

Similarities can also be found between nondualism and the monism at the roots of pre-Socratic western philosophy. Peter Kinglsey has written persuasively that the foundations of Western civilization were built from a direct and creative experience of oneness. Some argue that the message of nonduality can be found in the Gnostic Christian tradition. Many contemporary scientists find some common ground between the way the nondualistic perspective describes the universe and the way that quantum physics describes reality. There are, of course also many teachers and masters today who speak of nondual awareness with no reference to specific religious traditions, though most of them seem to have been informed by the study of one or more nondual spiritual traditions.

There is also a neo-advaitic strand of teaching and teachers that has either made Advaita Vedanta and the nonduality traditions of the East more accessible to Westerners or totally corrupted it through a series of accidental or deliberate misunderstandings (according to whom you are listening).

Of course that line isn't always straight. Sometimes there are

Waves.

Another way of picturing this line
is as the surface of an infinite ocean
of consciousness.

In this case GOD is the water—the ocean.

And,
you guessed it,
GOD is everything that is not the water as well.

The figure and ground paradox persists.

Musings:

 Does nonduality have a quality?

We live in a world that appears to be made up of physical things. We like to believe that those things are made of smaller things and those smaller things are made of still smaller things. While they may be extremely small, at some level we want to know that there are solid things and that they possess certain qualities independent of us and independent of our observation or participation.

But quantum physics suggests that at the level of the infinitely small, there are no things at all. There are only mathematical probabilities, and the qualities a thing seems to have are merely the reflection of the expectations of the observer.

Arising out of the recognition of the nondual nature of reality is the idea that the qualities a thing seems to possess do not exist, and in fact, cannot exist, independent of an observer. And since a separate observer is also an illusory construct, the best we can do is describe the way things seem to be.

This does not mean that things do not have qualities, only that there is nothing absolute we can say about them. We can have endless fascinating and even pleasurable conversations about how they seem as long as we don't assume that they are what they seem outside of those conversations.

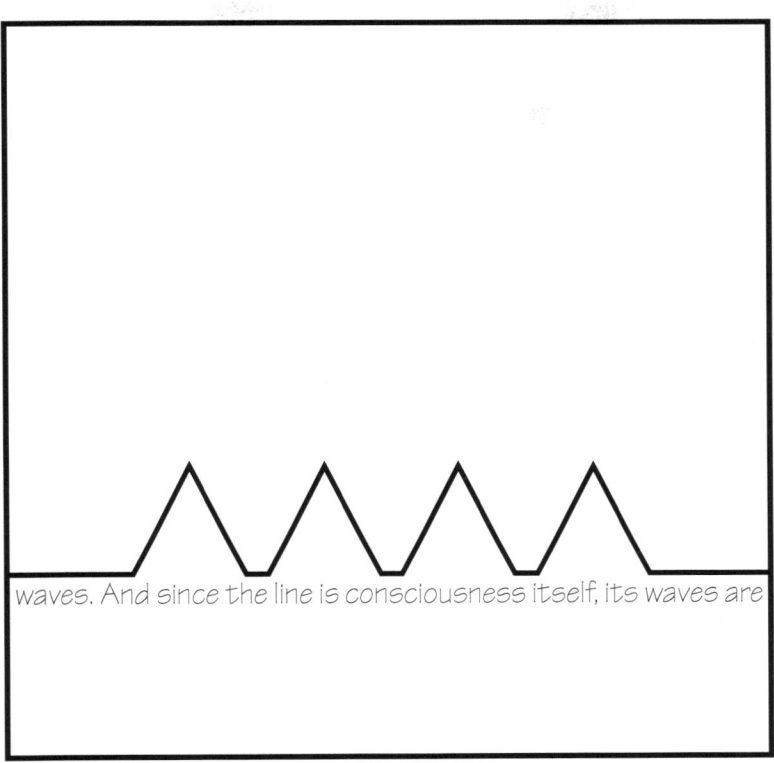

waves. And since the line is consciousness itself, its waves are

We don't really know why
GOD makes waves.

Perhaps it is play.

Perhaps "one" really is the loneliest number.

Perhaps forms allow GOD to know GOD.

Perhaps the figure ground paradox
is what waves are all about.

Musings:

 What role does attention play in recognizing the truth of nonduality?

For most of us, most of the time, attention feels like something that is beyond our control. Our attention is "captured" by external events or internal emotional states or sensations. We usually feel like we follow where our attention leads us. This contributes to the perception that the world of phenomena seems to be arising outside of us.

We have a choice. If we place our attention on the quality of separateness or distinction—this is this and that is that—we tend to imagine or perceive a world of separate and isolated forms.

We might say that it is better to place our attention on the quality of unification or oneness, but in nondual awareness separateness (the figure) and oneness (the ground) both collapse into their original state.

The traditions of meditation and contemplation and inquiry teach us that attention is a function which we can direct. The teaching technique known as the offering of "pointing-out" instructions (verbal clues or hints that nudge one into an awareness of the space between the thoughts) seems to work because it galvanizes our attention on what is actually happening in this moment.

Caught in the dreamscape of duality our attention is habitually attached to or attracted by form and the appearance of separation. But separation and oneness are simply qualities to which we are capable of attuning. We can attune to them because they are in us, <u>and</u> inherent in the things we are perceiving.

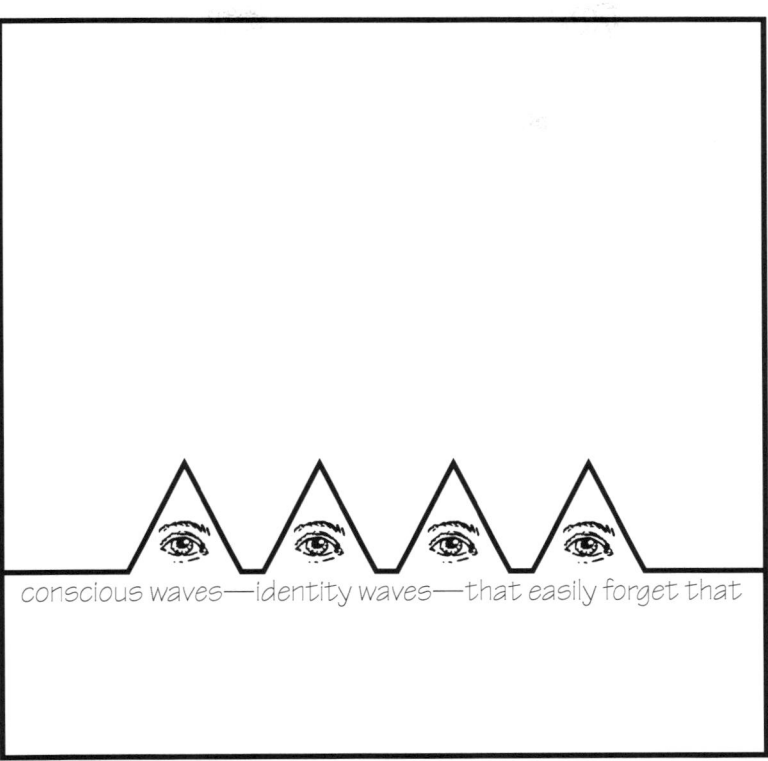

conscious waves—identity waves—that easily forget that

We don't know why there are waves,
but waves seem to arise.

They *seem* to be separate things
capable of perceiving other waves,
capable of acts of painful isolation and separation,
capable of acts of selfless surrender,
capable of bliss and capable of suffering,
capable of forgetting their very wave-ness,
sleepwalking from trough to crest,
and capable of awakening to their true nature.

The waves are us.

Musings:

 What happens when I pay attention?

Learning to place attention consciously is like learning to adjust the frequency receiver of a radio.

We all know that there are many channels on the radio broadcasting many different forms of sound. We also know that those sounds are interpenetrating us and all around us all of the time. The only reason we don't hear them is because we don't attune or attend to them.

Most of the time we live our lives as if our radio dials are stuck on the same station and we think "that station" is reality and that "that" is all there is. We hear a lot of songs (thoughts) we have heard before. We hear them so often that we come to believe that is what music (reality) actually is.

When we actually learn to direct our attention, as opposed to being directed by attention, our perception of reality expands. Simply expanding our awareness or sensitivity to the many frequencies of reality gives us more options. We learn to play the game of life (the illusion of appearances) with more artfulness and skill, but it does not mean that we wake up to the dream of the game.

Both meditative direction of attention and direct inquiry can lead to an awareness that everything we think of as being so solid and so real is simply a matter of the same stuff, vibrating at different speeds. While it may be that no practice will ever get you across the threshold of enlightenment (something we will discuss later), the practices of meditative direction of attention and direct inquiry will get you closer than any other practice.

their destiny is to dissolve...

Remember that there is only the line.
The line is GOD.
Every form is drawn from the same line.

If the line is GOD
and we are unique and temporary
expressions of the line
that rises up and dissolves
like waves on the ocean,
then we must be the waves
and the ocean at the same time.

We must be the figure and the ground.

Musings:

 ## What is the relationship between attention and form?

Is water (H2O) a solid, a liquid, or a gas?

Of course the answer is, it depends. Water exists as a liquid only within a narrow vibrational spectrum we call temperature.

When liquid vibrates slower than 32° Fahrenheit it begins to freeze and become solid. As ice, water is solid and powerful enough to tear open the hull of a steel ship.

When liquid vibrates faster than 32° Fahrenheit it begins to evaporate and become a gas. As steam, mist, or fog, water is nearly ephemeral.

Liquid, solid, and gas have very different qualities and they seem very different when you focus your attention on those qualities as they arise in each moment. And yet, if you bring your attention to the underlying commonality of substance, you can hold the awareness that they are both qualitatively distinct and, at the same time, simply the forms that water takes.

If your personal mythology dictates that steam is good and ice is bad, then you will suffer every time the temperature drops. You will develop elaborate life-strategies to keep water from freezing.

It isn't that your attention creates the forms that water takes, but your attention certainly writes the editorial in your mind about how you are "affected" by the form water is taking at the moment. Your narrowly focused attention can cause you to forget that ice, liquid, and steam are all the same substance vibrating at a different frequency. And, your expanded attention can help you remember the underlying oneness of form.

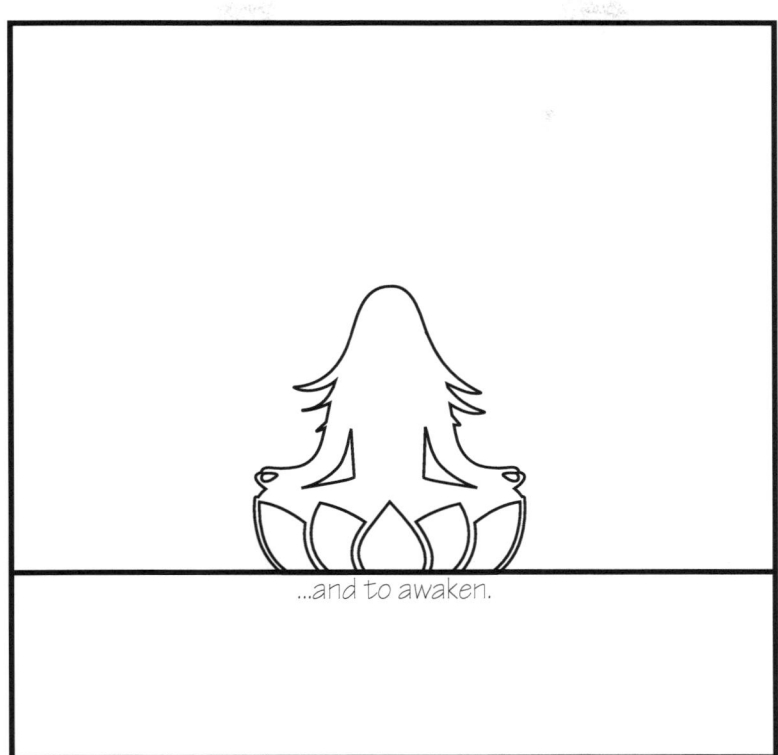

...and to awaken.

We are the line
that draws the wave,
that forgets the ocean.

We place our attention on the figure
and forget the ground
that we share with every form
that we are capable of perceiving.

It doesn't have to be this way,
but let's not get ahead of ourselves.

Chapter Two
The Something We Seem To Be

I seem to be a separate form
interacting with other separate forms,
clinging to an identity
like a drowning person clings
to a life preserver.

I seem to be a wave
bent on preserving my wave-ness
for as long as possible.

Musings:

 ## Something or nothing?

As tempting as it would be to bypass any discussion of the realm of form and appearances, I think it is important to begin in the realm of illusion, for no other reason than it is the collective dream that most of us are currently sharing.

It is also important because this ground of functional/dysfunctional form is where we all begin. We don't spontaneously get from the raw, unfiltered, nondual perspective of very early childhood to the experience of mature or transcendent awakening without becoming enchanted with and mesmerized by form. No one knows why this is, but it seems that no matter how close and how ever-present pure awareness is, we have to lose it before we can find it. Since the term and concept of the ego always arises in these discussions, let's begin with the distinction between a more psychological definition of ego and a more spiritual definition.

Psychological Definition: *The ego is the self-organizing principle in the psyche. It is literally the sense we have of an "I." It creates a sense of wholeness and integration. Without a healthy ego in good working order, a psychologist would deem us to be in bad shape.*

Spiritual Definition: *The ego is that emotional and psychological knot in consciousness that is the fundamental cause of the sense of separation from all life. It causes a constriction around a fixed identity that leads to a false sense of isolation and separation. The ego is seen as the cause of all suffering.*

Both of these definitions contain truth. The first feels true in the realm of form and the second feels true in the realm of formlessness. This chapter is a discussion of how things appear.

For some reason
that we do not really understand,
we seem to coagulate
out of the nothingness of dreamless sleep
into something that appears
solid and substantial and separate
every morning.

And, perhaps even more interesting
is the fact that the form that arises
is one which we seem to recognize.

Musings:

 Baby steps

How we seem to evolve.

When we are born, we are naturally very physical creatures. We are mostly a collection of physical sensations, vibrations, and perceptions that we respond to or express through particular behaviors like smiling, giggling, crying, staring, sleeping, etc. I say these are natural expressions of the body because they seem to be hard-wired into us. No one has to teach a baby how to laugh, or cry, or sleep, or stare in rapt curiosity and wonder.

Adults around us look at these physical forms of expression and attach meaning to them (or give them stories and labels, like she's sad, or he's happy). In time we <u>learn</u> to label our own forms of expression and to have judgments about them as well.

So from sensation and natural expressions of the body we develop what we call emotion or an emotional body or awareness. We have feelings, moods, impressions and intuitions that operate at or around the threshold between consciousness and subconsciousness.

These emotions or, more accurately, this movement in the emotional body seems to give rise to thoughts, concepts, theories, opinions, and ideas.

Or at least that's how it appears from this perspective.

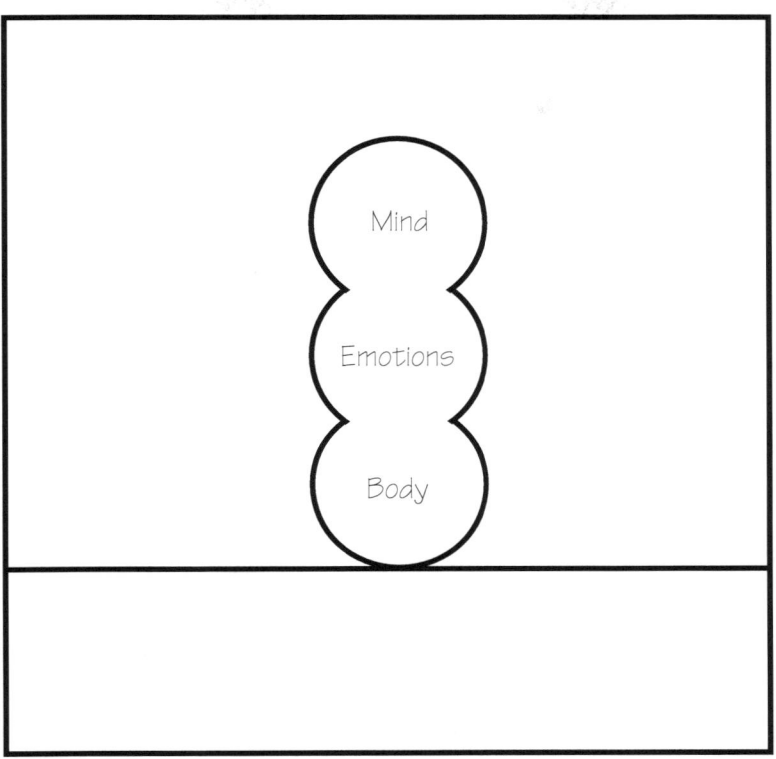

That form seems to be made up
of **MIND**
(thoughts, concepts, theories, opinions, ideas),
EMOTION
(feelings, moods, impressions, intuition,
and subconscious beliefs),
and **BODY**
(sensations, vibrations, perceptions).

The challenge is that rather than a sort of
"balanced snowman" form (above)...

Musings:

 Evolution

As animals, we are not well-adapted physically to survive. As animals, our triangles are probably almost all base or body with some feeling and intuition in the emotional body and virtually no thought or mind. If that is how we had stayed, we probably would not have survived or evolved.

But we didn't remain that way, we increased our capacity to think and use mind as a survival tool and strategy. Over time, those of us that survived, did so because we could better use our minds or our mental capacity and the mind began to play a greater role in our experience of being human.

As forms, forgetting for the moment that forms are illusory experiences, the amount of attention we place, moment-to-moment on the physical body, the emotional body, and the mental body, seems to impact our functionality. As forms, there are more functional forms and less functional forms.

In using the terms functional and dysfunctional I don't mean to imply a judgment so much as an observation that, even among forms with no apparent spiritual aspirations and no interest in enlightenment or awakening from the sleep walk of consensus reality, some forms function more effectively than others. We can take a form that allows us to exist more or less successfully in our social and cultural containers or we can take a form that intentionally or unintentionally causes those around us pain and ourselves suffering.

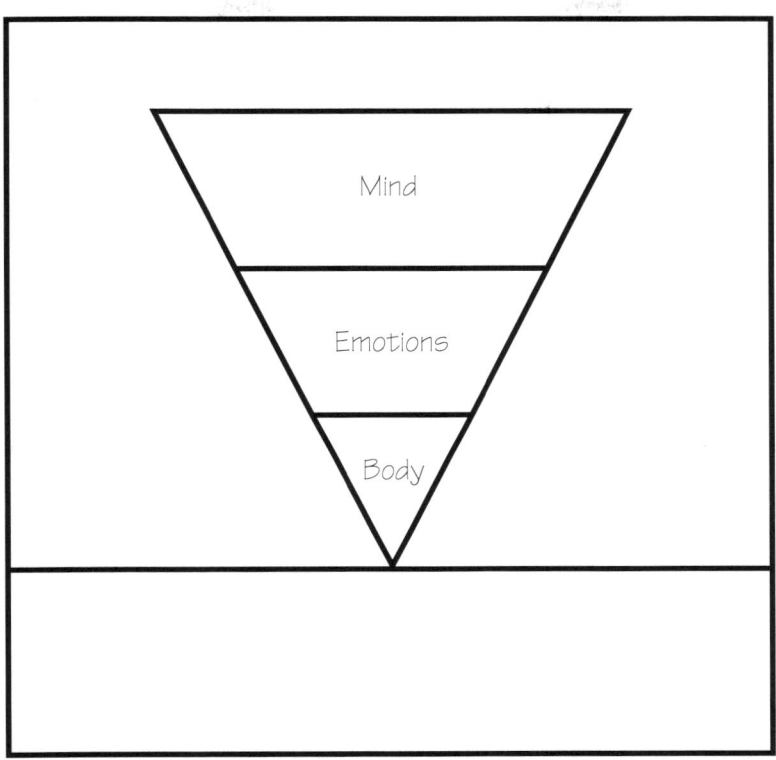

...we tend to take on an inverted triangle form.

This form is supported by the particular time and culture into which, most of us have been born.

We have been taught that pain and emotional states that cause us discomfort are bad and so we spend a lot of energy either distancing or distracting ourselves from pain or manipulating the external circumstances of our world.

Musings:

 Trauma and constriction

It is a common belief in our culture of appearances that we are the victims of the traumas of our past (especially our childhood) and that our behaviors can be largely attributed to those traumas. The real story is not that we are the result of our early traumas but that we are the sum total of our practices (both conscious and unconscious).

Some time in every one of our pasts, we were walking along breathing. We were happy, loving, open animals. Then, out of the blue we got punched in the stomach and it hurt. The moment after the punch (or trauma of any sort) we were the same person we were the moment before. The punch (trauma) didn't change us. What changed us was the practice (or story) that punch initiated. The moment after the punch, we clenched. We made some instinctive choice to never be caught off-guard like that again. We closed our hearts, tightened our muscles, armor-plated our most sensitive areas. I call this a practice because we had to have kept doing the practice with some intention (reinforcing it) until it became unconscious and second nature.

Each of us today is the result of a lifetime of unconscious practices. Our kinks and closures, our resistance and projections, are all things we once had to practice in order to feel safe. The process of unkinking and unconstricting requires practice as well. Initially this is very hard.

It is attractive (even seductive) to think that spirituality will allow us to make an end-run around the practice of unconstricting our illusory forms, but this usually just leads to kinked and constricted spiritual practitioners.

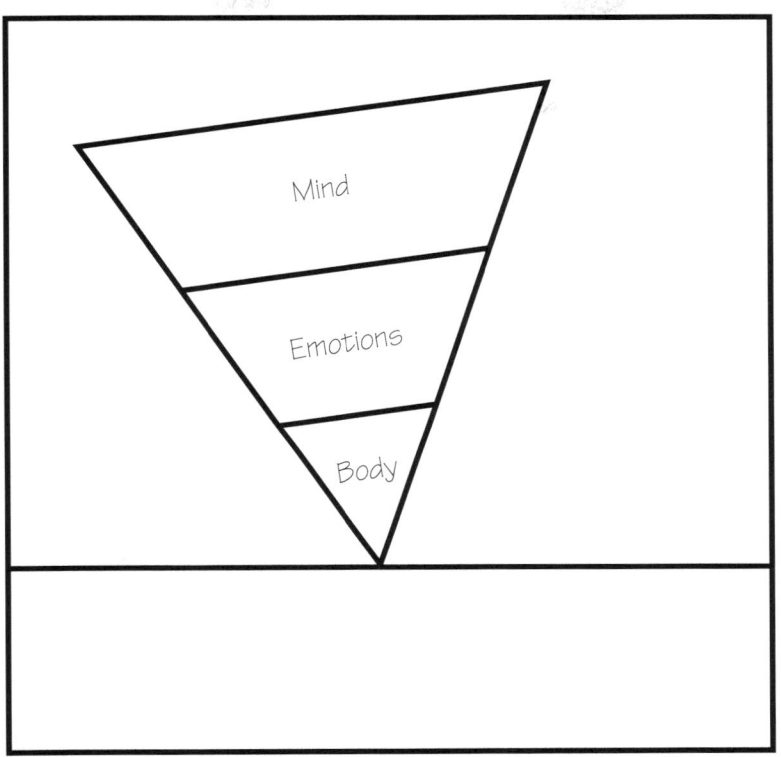

That gives us these unique inverted triangle shapes
in which our emotions and our bodies are
restricted and confined in the smallest space
like unruly animals.

We place great value on our
thoughts, ideas, opinions, concepts and theories—
the realm of mind.

We place almost no value
on the sensations, perceptions, and vibrations
that our bodies experience.

As you can see by the illustration above...

Musings:

 Dysfunctionality

It might seem foolish to spend time talking about functional versus dysfunctional illusions (forms). For one thing, why worry about dysfunctional forms? Wouldn't a dysfunctional form more quickly discover its own illusory nature? And if functional and dysfunctional are both illusory forms anyway, why bother talking about either of them?

The truth is that functional and dysfunctional still matter in this realm for several reasons. For one thing, dysfunctional forms do not recognize their own illusory nature more easily. They are as stubborn as they are unstable. They continually crash and continually rebuild themselves on old dysfunctional models. They are locked into their sense of separateness and so always see their crashes and their dysfunction as being caused by things exterior to themselves.

If the <u>idea</u> of spiritual enlightenment or pure awareness or nonduality manages to gain a foothold in their consciousness, they are far more likely to use those "concepts" to attempt to bypass their dysfunctionality and create a new ego identity as a spiritual seeker or an enlightened person.

It is tempting to romanticize dysfunction and even make it into some marker for spiritual evolution, but I think it would be very difficult to find an enlightened being who knowingly causes others pain. And I am clearly differentiating between pain and suffering here. Pain is something we do seem to have the capacity to inflict upon others, as opposed to suffering, which we do not. Pain is something that happens to us in this incarnation. Suffering is just one of the responses to suffering that we have available to us. Where pain is an event, suffering is a choice.

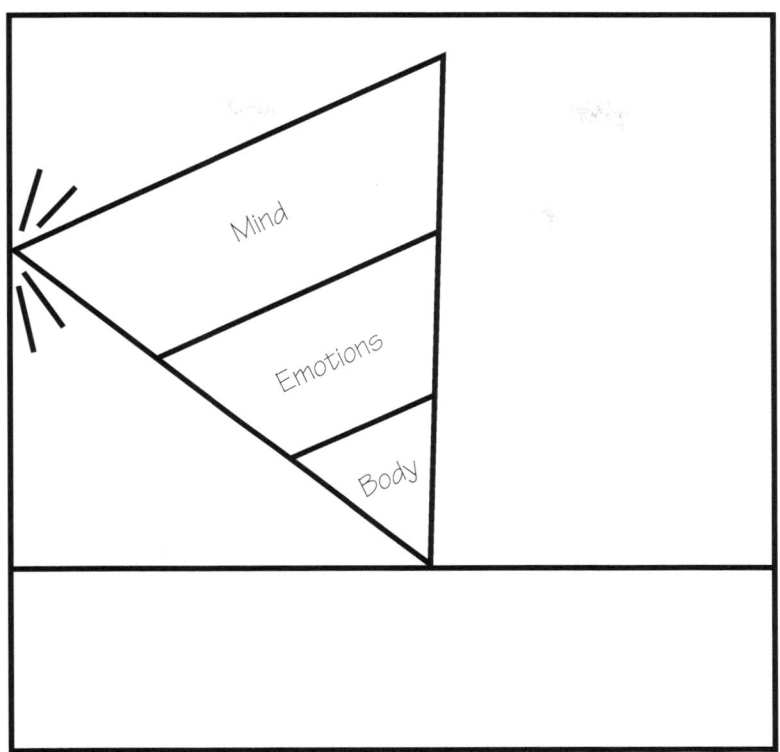

...this form is not particularly stable.

It collapses easily,
is destabilized by the subtlest of movement,
reaches overwhelm by the slightest of stresses,
and clings desperately to anything
that props up the structures of separate identity.

This form is what we might call dysfunctional.
This is not a judgment, but rather an observation.
It means that the form causes others pain
and the self largely unnecessary suffering.

This form is also not very wave-like.

Musings:

 Suffering and prepared ground

While both functional forms and dysfunctional forms can have rigid boundaries, the combination of rigid boundaries and in-stability is particularly problematic when it comes to spiritual growth and evolution. Dysfunctional forms are disconnected forms. When they experience overload and overwhelm, they break down instead of breaking through. They do not have the stability to maintain their ground and stand in the transfor-mative fire long enough break through to some higher order of organization.

While it is tempting to hypothesize about dysfunctional forms simply having spiritual awakenings that reveal the true nature of reality and end their dysfunction, it is difficult to find exam-ples of it. A few apocryphal stories aside, actual enlightenment seems to favor maturity and functionality.

In this realm, examples of awakening almost always occur with some combination of great suffering and prepared ground. The great suffering seems necessary in order to really understand that no strategy is going to alleviate the pain you are feeling. No identity or egoic "fix" is going to return you to a romanticized past or a fantasized future state of happiness. And prepared ground, through some form of mindfulness training, ruthless self-awareness, penetrating self-inquiry, or spiritual practice under the direction of a master, seems necessary for suffering to be transmuted into anything more than just more suffering.

It has been said that enlightenment is an accident, but that meditation (or certain other spiritual practices) make one ac-cident prone.

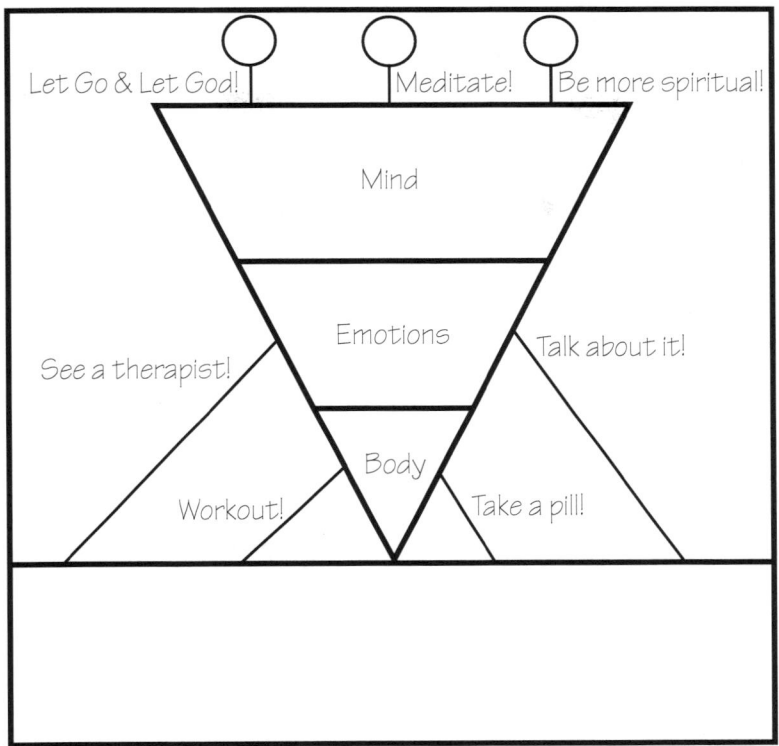

This inverted triangle form
requires stabilization.

We tend to stabilize with physiological approaches
like pharmaceuticals and exercise,
psycho-emotional approaches
like talk-therapy and shadow work,
or spiritual approaches
like meditation, compassion and
devotional spirituality.

Each of these approaches is useful but incomplete
in themselves and, when relied upon
as the one answer, dangerous.

Musings:

 The role of therapy

So, while the inverted triangle model of awareness may have plenty of suffering to qualify as preparation for awakening, it usually anesthetizes or distracts itself from the suffering, which eliminates its potential for transformation, and it almost never has the prepared ground upon which suffering might be transformed. Which brings us to therapy.

At about the time that science overtook religion as the dominant paradigm for understanding the world and our place in it, we adopted the idea of therapy. Therapy is actually an adaptation of the idea that practice and mastery can be applied to physical, emotional, and psychological states.

In its early days, therapy was designed to cultivate functionality (usually as defined by a cultural or social norm). In the latter half of the 20th century, as Western therapies bumped up against Eastern spiritual practices, transcendental forms of therapy emerged that blended righting the inverted triangle (for enhanced functionality) with a goal that seemed to suggest something beyond functionality. Even today, there are branches of therapy and counseling that rely on a nondual perspective in order to address suffering.

Most baby boomers with an interest in self-growth have had more than a passing exposure to at least one form of therapy. When it comes to therapy, it is common to hear the phrase "I've done therapy," or "I've done my work." This usually means that a person has had some degree of therapy to address some of the major areas of constriction and woundedness in their lives. It can mean that one has moved from dysfunctionality to functionality in some areas of life. Unfortunately, it is epidemic in many forms of contemporary and even classical spirituality to bypass therapy in favor of "spiritual" work.

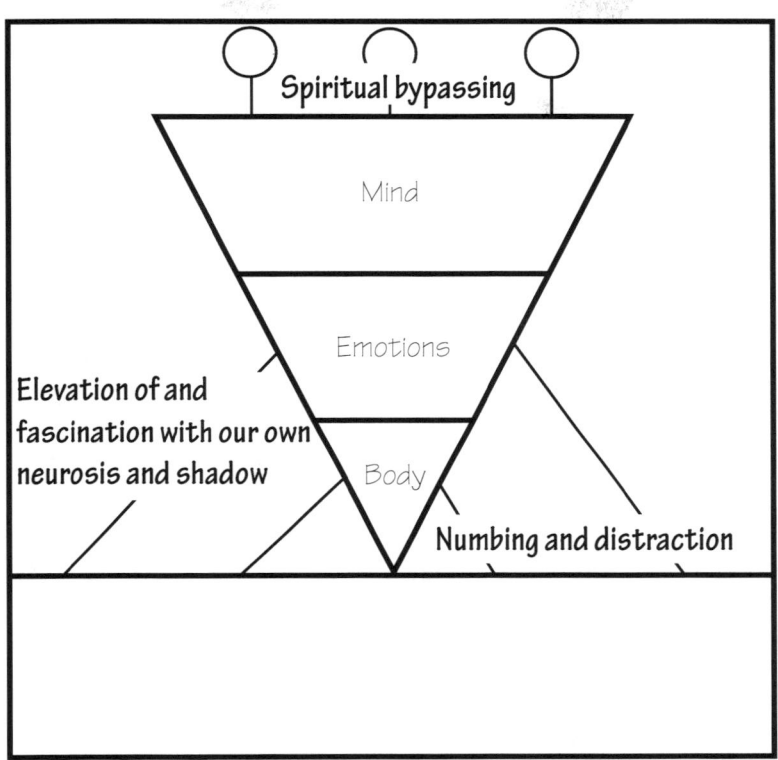

Body centered and pharmaceutical approaches
alone tend to lead to numbing and distraction.
When stressed, we raise the dosage or "do" more.

Pyscho-emotional solutions alone can trap us in
endless fascination with our own shadow
and subconscious identity struggles.
We understand why we are doing
what we are doing, but we keep doing it.

Spiritual approaches alone tend to lead
to spiritual bypassing. We repress shadow
and restrict the expression of energy to what is
acceptable for a "spiritual" person.

Musings:

 Therapy and constriction

I'm going to continue to play with the metaphor of the physical body for a moment, but I am talking about emotional trauma and constriction as well as physical trauma and constriction.

When we contract and hold muscles in a limited and tense position for a long time, they become rigid and inflexible. Eventually we may experience pain in those areas or referred pain in other areas that compensate for the constant tension. That pain or rigidity is something we are doing to ourselves in the present moment. That person who caused us pain all those years ago, did a hurtful thing and this is not about transferring blame. We were not asking to be hurt. We did not cause the pain. But the suffering we feel today is something we are doing to ourselves.

Usually other people can see this more clearly than we can. There is a tendency to give the easy advice—"relax," or "let it go," but that is usually frustrating and ineffective. We've been constricted so long that we no longer remember that we are constricting ourselves. We've lost any sense of where the on/off switch for that muscle group is. A good physical therapist will often ask us to tense those muscles even more, rather than just tell us to relax them. It is only by tensing those muscles (which often hurts like hell) that we relearn how to relax them and remember that we have any control over them at all.

The therapeutic and sometimes even the spiritual practices we do are designed to help us remember that we are the ones doing the constricting and the kinking around our capacity to flow with love as light or as consciousness. A good practice, if it is really helping us loosen a deeply held constriction, is going to hurt like hell.

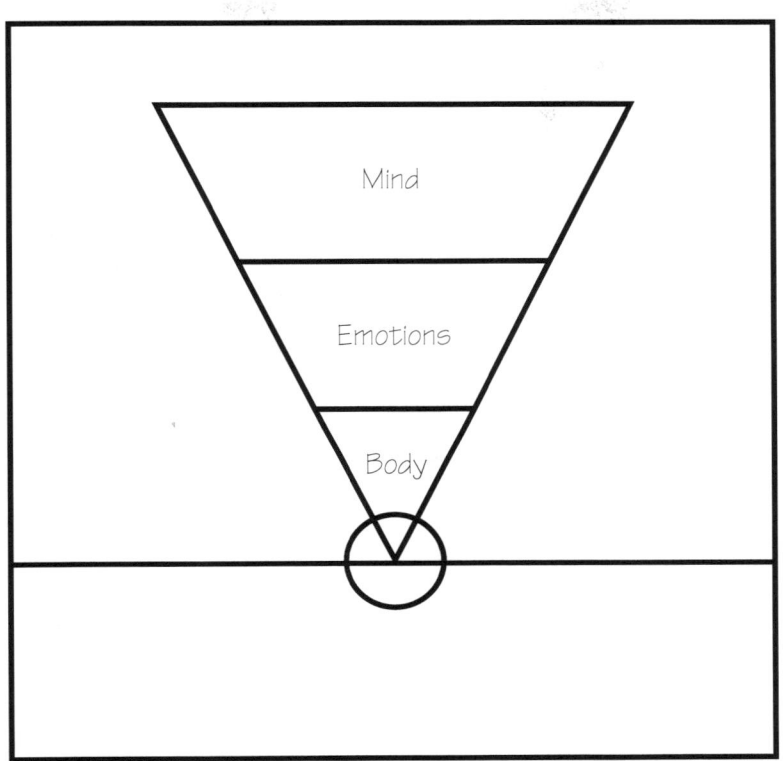

This inverted triangle form
requires a highly constricted sense
of our connectedness to GOD or oneness
(that line with which we are all drawn).

In order to conceive of or imagine ourselves
as these inverted triangles,
we have to cut ourselves off from GOD
and from each other
and we end up as unstable,
separate and lonely beings,
balancing tenuously in continuous anxiety.

Musings:

 Therapy and happiness

Most people would describe themselves as looking for some kind of happiness. Initially we all tend to see happiness as coming from an external state change (the acquisition of objects of desire or finding the perfect relationship or situation). At some level, many people begin to realize that there are internal barriers to their ability to experience the happiness they desire. At this point they either turn to therapy or to therapeutic forms of spirituality.

Happiness means different things to people but there is at least one definition in which happiness means a sense of or capacity to "abide with" or "be at peace with." It is a relaxation or cessation from the struggle to change one's state of being. If I receive news or have an experience that evokes sadness or anger, my challenge is to be with that feeling without repressing it, without judging it, and without distracting myself from it by fantasizing about when it will go away and when I will feel differently.

The paradox here, which I will state over and over again, is that the desire for a different state or a different future is both the motivation to practice being present with what arises and releasing our attachment to outcomes, <u>and</u> the barrier to ultimately being in that state. Desire is that life preserver that keeps us alive and practicing toward a fully integrated awakened state <u>and</u> it is that thing we cling to when what we finally need to do is let go and dissolve in the ocean of oneness.

So therapy and therapeutic forms of spirituality can be both a help and a hindrance.

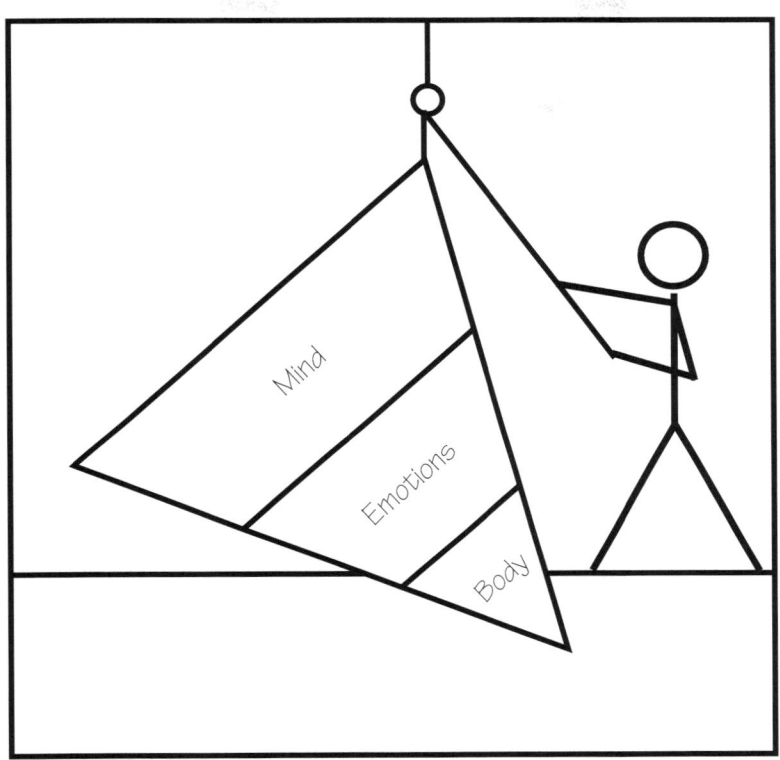

Certain therapies address this dysfunction
by addressing the form and construction
of our psyches through inversion.

They promote the return to a kind of primacy
of the physical sensations perceived by the body,
with the mind playing the role of subtle guide
rather than megalomanic dictator.

Musings:

 Functionality

Therapy can be highly effective at helping people recognize their shadows, their projections, their habitual patterns, and their subconscious or unconscious dysfunctional routines.

The relationship between therapy and enlightenment is, according to some teachers, very clear. All therapy is just an adjustment that perpetuates an illusion. But in the realm of form there is a spectrum of functionality that therapy and spiritual practice can and do address.

Dysfunctionality *is a state in which we are living constricted and closed lives that are well-defended and very locked into rigidly separate egoic consciousness. From this position we create pain for others and suffering for ourselves, sometimes consciously and sometimes without consciousness.*

Functionality *is a state that may be less constricted and less closed, but is primarily indicated by the fact that we no longer knowingly cause others pain and actively try to reduce the amount of suffering we take on. Therapy for functionality addresses how we play the game without addressing the nature of the game itself.*

Hyper-functionality *is when we are better than we need to be at a particular thing. If functionality equals acceptable performance, hyper-functionality means mastery. Of course, one can be functional or hyper-functional in certain areas of development (spiritual intelligence, emotional intelligence, artistic intelligence, ethical or moral intelligence, etc.) without having that level of functionality transfer to other areas. That is one of the challenges of spiritual teachers and gurus. They can be hyper-functional in spiritual development and barely functional or even dysfunctional in moral/ethical development.*

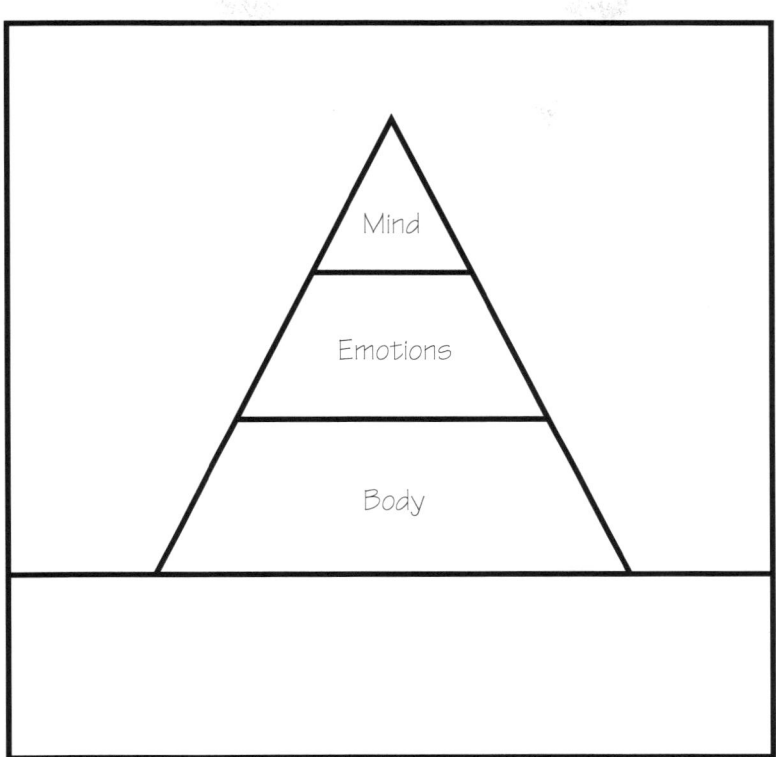

And this rebalanced triangle is indeed
more functional, more resourceful,
more stable, and more solid.

It is more wave-like and,
because it is not so cut-off and alienated,
it tends to play well with the other waves.

This then is success in the realm of functionality.
It is the goal and the limit of most therapies.
It is the healthy functioning egoic structure that
society and social structures seem to need.

End of story.

Musings:

 Trans-functionality

So if someone came to me with a problem of dysfunctionality in relationship, meaning that they were causing their intimate partner a great deal of pain and causing themselves a lot of suffering, I would suggest therapy to move them from dysfunctionality to functionality.

If someone came to me with a functional relationship and wanted to go further into the art and energetic mastery of intimate relationship (meaning they wanted to be better than they needed to be), I might suggest a physically or spiritually-based practice like tantra to move into the realm of hyper-functionality. If they practiced with consistency, they would eventually master the art of sexual or physical intimacy, but they could do this and still be as locked into an egoic identity as someone who was merely functional (just look at the contemporary or neo-tantric community). The mastery that comes with hyper-functionality, whether one has mastered sexual intimacy or meditation or the piano, does not necessarily take one any closer to the truth of reality—the pure awareness of nonduality.

Now where this gets tricky is in the urge toward trans-functionality. **Trans-functionality** *goes beyond the concerns of functionality and even of hyper-functionality. It can even look at moments as if it is dysfunctional from a social or cultural perspective, but it is actually no longer concerned with functionality at all.*

If someone comes to me and wants to transcend their separate sense of self and dissolve the barriers that constantly reinforce egoic identity, I might offer what appear to be practices, even though I know that these practices will actually do nothing but prepare the ground and that no practices will actually carry one across the threshold from illusion to truth.

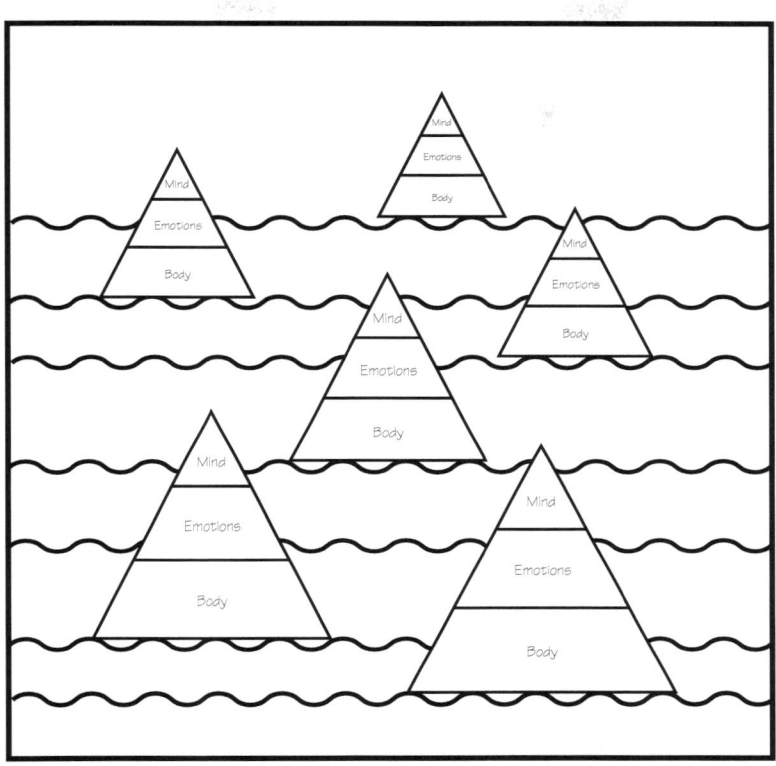

Or is it?

Many spiritual teachers,
especially those of the nondual persuasion,
would say that this ocean of happy triangles
is just another layer of illusion.

Chapter Three
The Divine Tremor

In moments, my separateness
seems to dissolve.

My wave-ness stills
and seems to resolve itself back
into an infinite ocean of being.

Musings:

 Something and nothing

This chapter is an exercise in even more foolishness.

The right hand pages are a visual exploration of a theory about the relationship between something and nothing. No one really needs this theory, and yet, in the realm of form (where most of us spend most of our time) there is a great deal of confusion in the borderlands between "doing" and "not doing," between the desire for growth and change and the recognition that all is perfect as it is.

There is a famous Zen saying that goes, "Before enlightenment, chop wood and carry water. After enlightenment, chop wood and carry water."

What intrigues me is what is the relationship between enlightenment and chopping wood and carrying water. If I am particularly dangerous at chopping wood and particularly inept at carrying water, will enlightenment change that? If enlightenment means that I stop dwelling in the recollected past or the anticipated future (in my remembered failures and projected fantasies of failing) when it comes to chopping or carrying, that seems like a good thing. On the other hand, if I use it as an excuse to avoid improving my capacity to chop wood without losing body parts or carrying water without wasting most of it because "everything is perfect as it is," that seems like a denial of the actual experience of being born into this realm.

There is a nondual or pure awareness and then there are ideas about nonduality. Unfortunately, these ideas about nonduality can be taken to an extreme, as can any idea. What follows is a model of the relationship between the realm of form and the realm of formlessness (which admittedly sounds very dualistic and I haven't even begun yet).

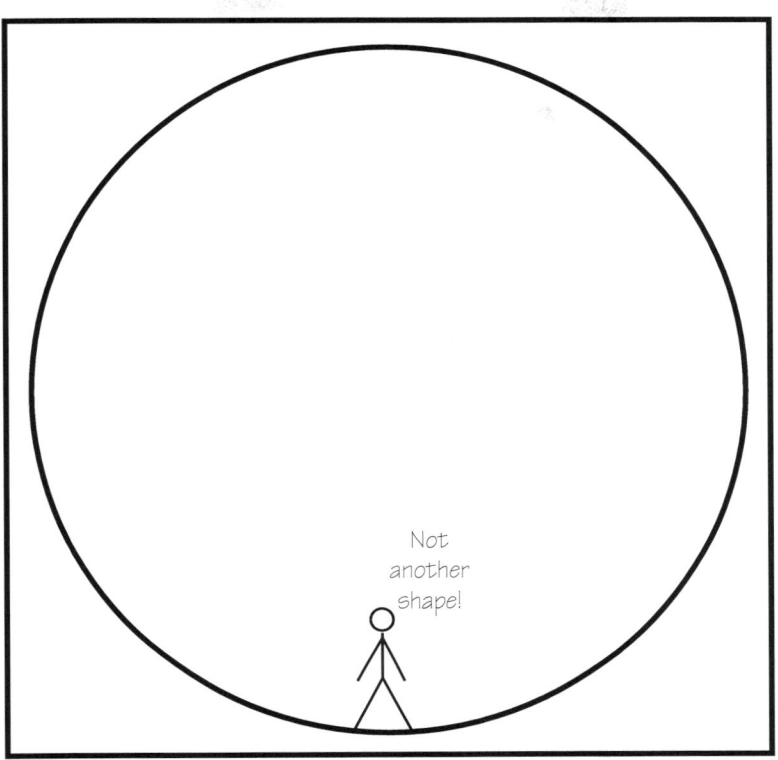

Some religions and some spiritual teachers
suggest that the triangle shape
(remember that ocean of happy triangles?)
is just a temporary and illusory form that
consciousness takes.

Our true nature is actually a field
or a pool of pure consciousness.

We'll illustrate it as a circle,
but it is not really different
from the empty square or the infinite line
we have been using.

Musings:

 Nondual irony

Nonduality or pure awareness is, as I have mentioned before, such a strange concept to a world steeped in the myth of separation that the best way to approach it is to circle it in a spiraling motion, coming ever closer to its radical heart.

In this spiral dance, it is ironic that we start out describing two different ways that people speak of nonduality. While everyone agrees that nonduality transcends qualities, Different schools of thought speak of it in ways that sound very different.

Some teachers describe nonduality as the quality of union— the dissolution of form into the ultimate reality of God, the absolute, love. This quality is something we can pursue or to which we can aspire. It is something that is knowable and can be gained via the practice of meditation, and inquiry and the appropriate means of knowledge. This form of nonduality is described in blissful and peaceful terms, characterized by equanimity, as if a stormy ocean had finally come to rest.

The second quality is beyond union, is not knowable and is a state that is not attainable without annihilating every aspect of separate self (ego) that would be there to perceive its attainment. It requires the long, dark night of the soul. It is the leap into the unknown. It can be horrifying. It is described in terms that alternate between fiery oblivion and the deep dark emptiness of the void. It is the mystery.

Perhaps it is both at the same time. Perhaps awakening is as simple as a recognition and as challenging as a leap off a sheer cliff into the darkness.

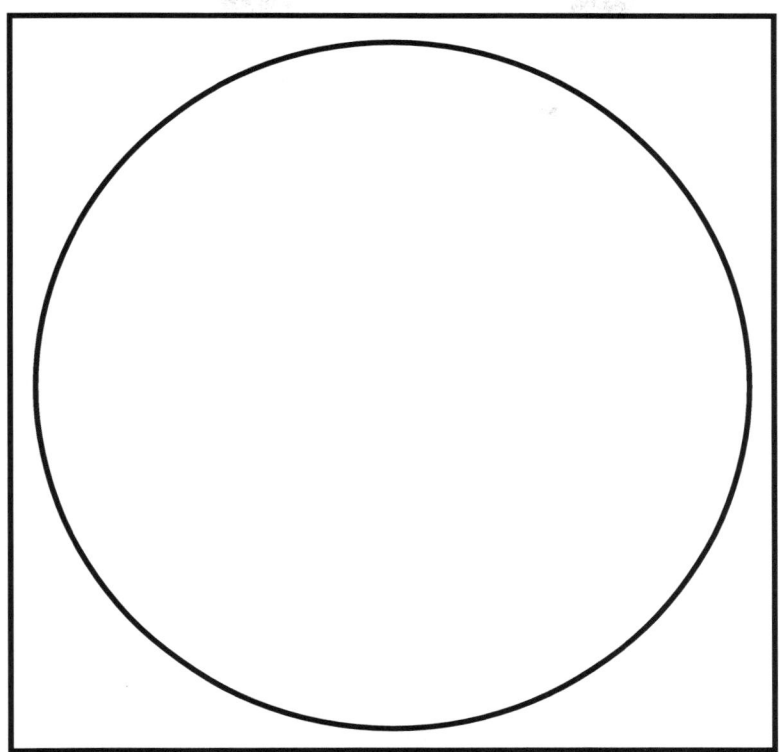

This circle is possibility.
It is ever-present, undifferentiated, nondual
consciousness.
It is the ground or ocean of being.
Another word for this is space.

It is unmanifest or infinitely manifested.
At this moment it makes no difference.

This is GOD awake as GOD.

This is also you and me.

Musings:

 Sleepwalking

Like many spiritual commentators, I use the word sleepwalking to describe the state of dualistic separation we find ourselves in. We look like we are awake, but we aren't. If we were awake we would know the truth. I also like the word sleepwalking because we don't judge people for sleepwalking. We don't hold them responsible for what they do when they are sleepwalking. And, in the end, it doesn't make much difference whether someone is sleepwalking because their parents or culture never taught them to distinguish the difference between awake and asleep. The reasons don't matter. It's still sleepwalking.

When I am sleepwalking through life, the "inner temper tantrum" runs me. It dictates my external actions. Of course, it might not be an inner temper tantrum, It might be an inner sense of failure or unworthiness, but when I feel that feeling, I want to disown it or distract myself from it. I want to project it onto others and make them responsible for it. I know how absurd this is and yet it is what the sleepwalking me wants.

There is a quote from Wayne Dyer that I have always liked:
  "If you take an orange and squeeze it and say, What will come out? …well, it's orange juice, because it's an orange. That what's inside. If someone squeezes you—puts pressure on you, says something you don't like—out of you comes anger, hatred, bitterness, anxiety, tension, fear, stress. But it's not because of who or what did the squeezing. It's because that's what's inside."

There is also a quote from Rilke that comes to mind: "Be patient with all that is unsolved in your heart and try to love the questions themselves." *When it comes to pure awareness, the questions are sometimes more important than the answers.*

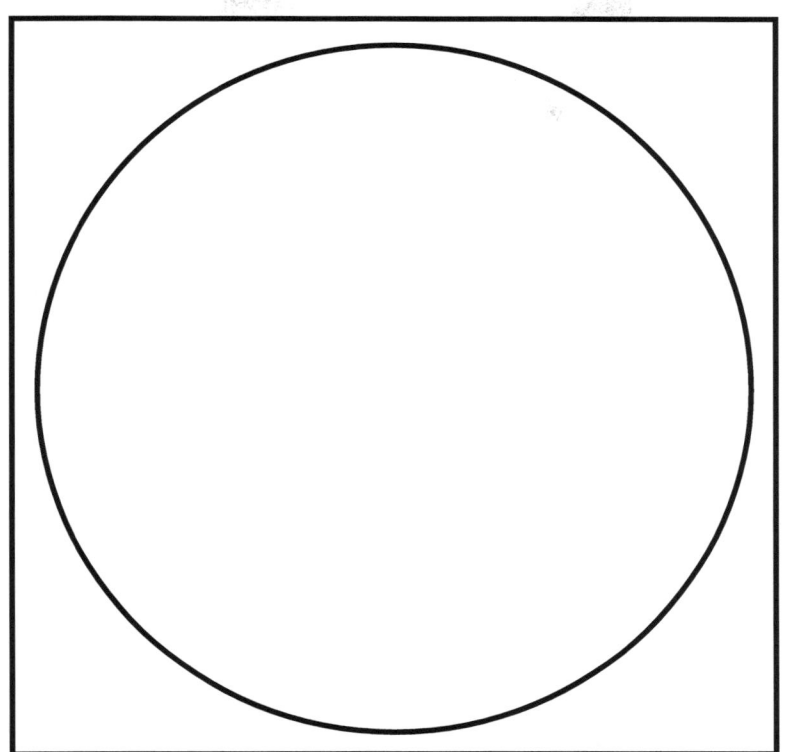

But GOD awake as GOD cannot know GOD.

It simply is GOD.

In order for consciousness to know itself
or see itself, it must differentiate into form.

Without form there can be no experience.

Why does GOD care
whether there is experience or not?

No one knows.
It's a mystery.

Musings:

 The questions:
What is this dissatisfaction I feel?

We have described GOD or consciousness or the oneness with several metaphors. We have called it the line from which we are all drawn, the ocean from which we all arise as temporary wave forms, and the divine tremor that plays across the infinite pool of conscious space.

For whatever reason, the journey of our incarnation in this realm seems to be one of placing our attention on the figure rather than the ground, the waves rather than the ocean, the tremor rather than the pool. We imagine ourselves to be separate and isolated selves haunted by a vague sense of lost intimacy that we can never satisfy.

This means that we never have the complete picture We are trapped in a kind of longing for wholeness that we interpret as needing things or people or circumstances to resolve. But no matter how much we acquire, that ache never goes away. It may be stilled for awhile, but it always returns (we explore this in more detail in chapter four).

Our seeking may become more sophisticated. We may shift from seeking material goods and fame and power to seeking the ideal relationship with another, to seeking spiritual peace and wholeness, but it is all still seeking, and it will never quiet that longing we have to return home.

The irony is that home is always ever-present. We don't need to go anywhere or do anything to find it.

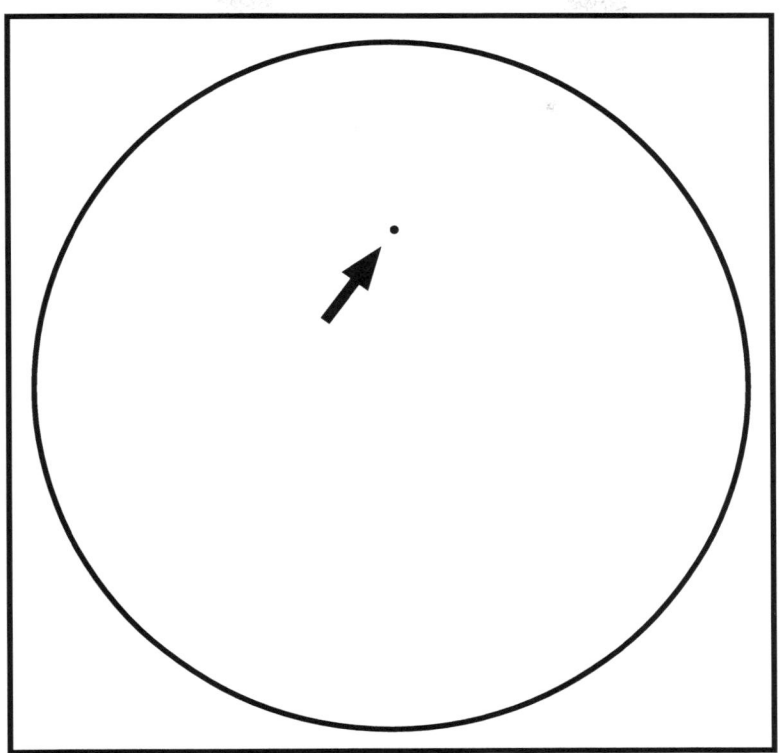

This is GOD dreaming.

This the big bang.
This is the singularity.
This is the genesis.
This is the seed.

These are all metaphors
for talking about a mystery
that is beyond our comprehension.

Somehow a drop falls.
A single splash of vibration creates something
where a moment before there was nothing.

Musings:

 The questions:
Do I need to believe in nonduality?

You don't have to believe in gravity in order not to float off into space. You don't have to believe in air in order to breathe successfully. And you don't have to believe that we are all one and that nothing exists that isn't God or that we are God in order to understand that the responsibility for your happiness rests with you. You could see it from a purely practical perspective: How much control do you have over what other people do and think and say? How much control do you have over the events that unfold each day. You may think you have a lot of control, but, in reality you have no control.

And the very fact that you believe you need control means that you are causing your own suffering as you run around trying to change or fix other people or control events so that life will unfold the way you think you want it to.

Sometimes, in small ways, controlling our external circumstances seems to work. But all of us have spent enough time in our lives trying that strategy without much success. We are never happy for long, because we always carry the tension that someone or something else is going to rise up that we will need to control. The path to sanity (to awakening) seems to be to take responsibility for ourselves. This does not need to be a spiritual truth. It functions on a purely intellectual or philosophical level.

Few people actually want the kind of world shattering experience that is enlightenment. However the truth that is revealed in even a momentary state of enlightenment (the one taste of nondual awareness) can lessen the need to defend our separate sense of self.

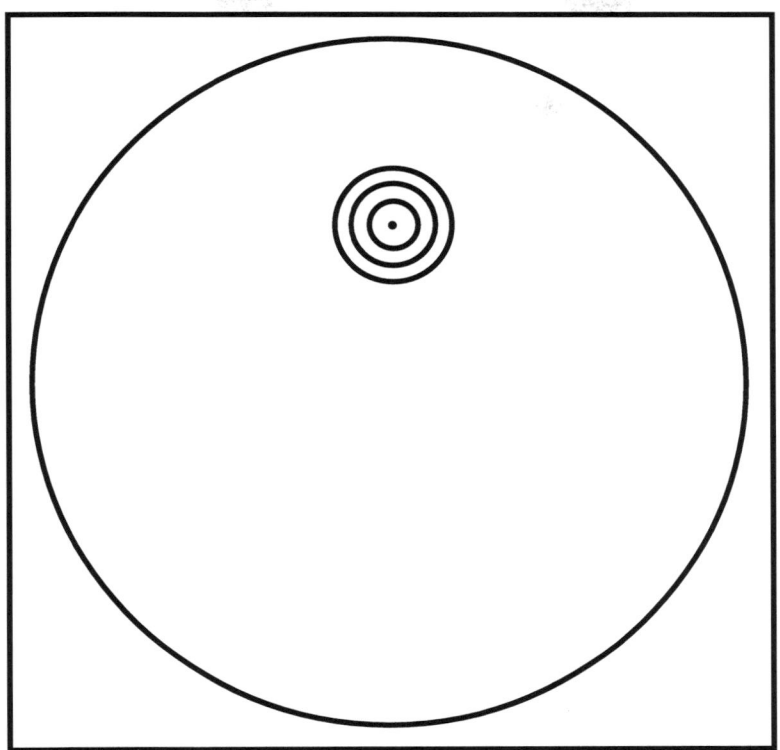

Differentiation begins in the ground or space
of consciousness through vibration,

In Sanskrit there is a word,
spanda.

It means divine tremor.
The divine tremor is the beginning of form.

It is the seed of what will become you and me and
all the other waves of apparently separate
and unique beings.

It is energy dancing in empty space.

Musings:

 The questions:
I had a profound experience of oneness
once. Does that mean I'm enlightened?

Experiencing the state of oneness, that one taste of pure aware-
ness can be profound and even life-changing, but it is a state
change as opposed to a developmental stage change. Ken Wil-
ber writes about this in much more detail in books such as,
"One Taste" *and **"Integral Spirituality,"** but what is most im-*
portant to know is that a change in our state of consciousness
can happen at any time, with no preparation and no specific
training.

We can have an overwhelming sense of the dissolution of our
own separate identity and the underlying oneness of all form
through psycho-active drugs and plant medicines, through
intense sexual union, by exposure to highly charismatic indi-
viduals who have a gift for taking people into that state ex-
perience, through intense meditation, sensory deprivation,
and even near-death experiences. On the positive side, these
tastes can give us the motivation to truly wake up—a glimpse
of the territory from outside of the dream. On the negative side,
these tastes are fleeting and we often just add them to the list
of experiences we are seeking more of. We come to believe that
mushrooms or orgasms or shaktipat hurling gurus or intense
spiritual practices are the necessary path to awakening.

Ken Wilber has also suggested that while we can experience
a change in our <u>state</u> of consciousness from any <u>stage</u> of con-
sciousness, we can only understand or interpret it after the fact
from our current developmental <u>stage</u> of consciousness. So, a
state change experience of oneness from a lower stage of con-
sciousness might trigger a lifetime of spiritual seeking for some-
thing that is already ever-present and only a breath away.

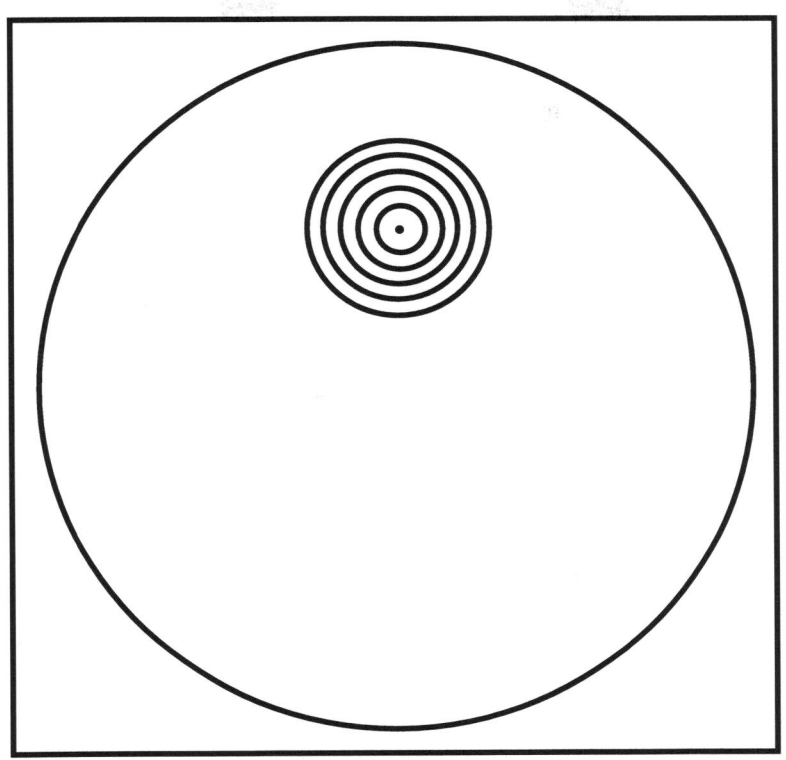

It is pure vibration.
And vibration, it turns out,
is the only thing can actually be perceived.

Perhaps that is because we recognize ourselves in
everything else that vibrates.

Perhaps vibration is simply the organizing
principle of our wave-ness,
the pattern or scaffolding
upon which our wave-ness manifests.

Musings:

 The questions:
So are there degrees of enlightenment?

Absolutely not! You are either awake or not awake. Or...

It depends on how you understand what is happening.

Some people who have written or spoken of their experiences have described a sudden dropping away of all sense of a separate self that was dramatic and permanent. On one side was separation and suffering and on the other side was oneness and peaceful abiding. Of course that usually occurs after some significant preparation or a traumatic breakdown of some sort. That would suggest that enlightenment is an either/or experience with only an on and off switch.

Other, equally credible individuals have described a similar singular experience of oneness followed by a kind of integration period in which this new awareness needed to settle in and stabilize. It is characterized by a kind of on again/off again awareness with an increasing amount of time spent in the on state. This would suggest that awakening can be a kind of rheostat experience, dialed up to full and stabilized awareness over some period of time.

In Kashmir Shaivism there is a spectrum of what liberation is, when it occurs, and what is required to attain it. There is a form that is instant, bestowed by Shiva directly, and results in the instant death of the physical body (not much fun there). There is also a version that eliminates all ignorance and you don't have to die to abandon duality. Then there are lesser versions that can be bestowed by a guru and result in liberation in your next life or after some other suitable waiting period.

Sounds like the kind of thing about which people could argue endlessly.

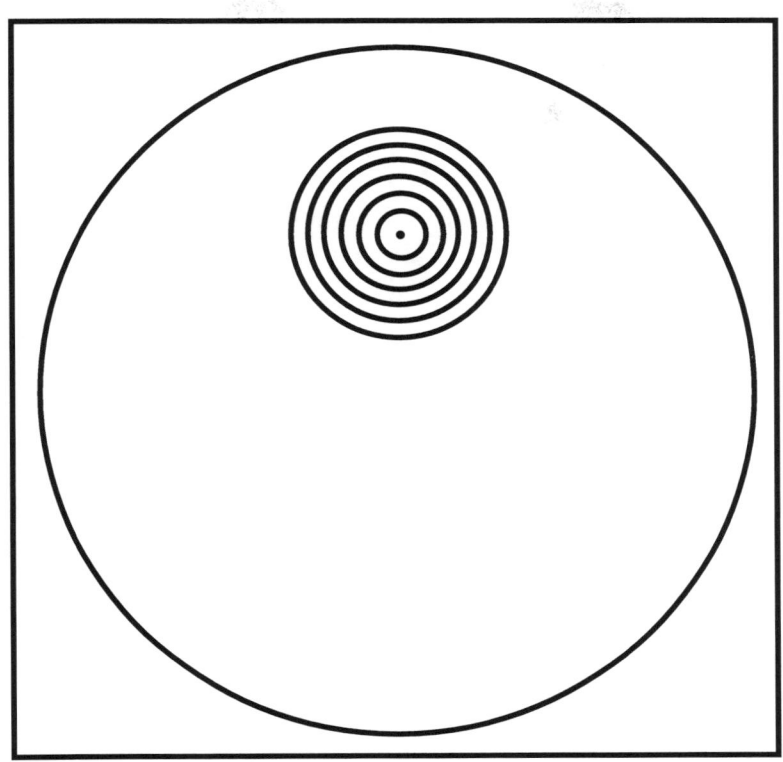

From the moment of that one drop,
that divine tremor,
we are in the realm of duality.

Emptiness and Form
Space and Energy.
Stillness and Vibration.

But notice
that I am not saying there are two things.
There is still only one thing

Musings:

 The questions:
Why is waking up so difficult?

My sense of myself as a unique and separate being or form is an illusion. It has to be. Whether you understand this from a metaphysical perspective—it's all GOD, or from a mathematical perspective—it's all probabilities, or from a scientific perspective—it's all the vibration of space, there is nothing to support the idea that separate forms are anything but an appearance, a construction, an illusion. This illusion feels very real, but so does the world we dream at night when we sleep.

"I" is an identity that has been constructed out of thoughts and feelings and experiences. We are all alive today, from the perspective of a genetic and biological story, because our ancestors made better choices in terms of physical survival or evolved better instinctive survival mechanisms.

Just as our physical forms might seem to have physical survival preferences, our egos (our sense of "I" as embodied beings) have survival instincts. It is these identity survival instincts that keep us stuck in the dream of separation. Peak experiences of oneness bypass or override these survival mechanisms and reveal a glimpse of the truth of our oneness with all beings, but it can be very difficult to shake that illusion or awaken from the dream of separation because our identity survival mechanisms are so strong.

The reason why enlightenment is sometimes described as horrifying is that our identities perceive enlightenment as death, which, in fact it is, from the perspective of a separate and unique identity. Our identities do not surrender their defenses quietly. Every story we have about ourselves, everything we think "we" are, will be seen as just an illusion, but we've spent a good part of our lives building and reinforcing that illusion.

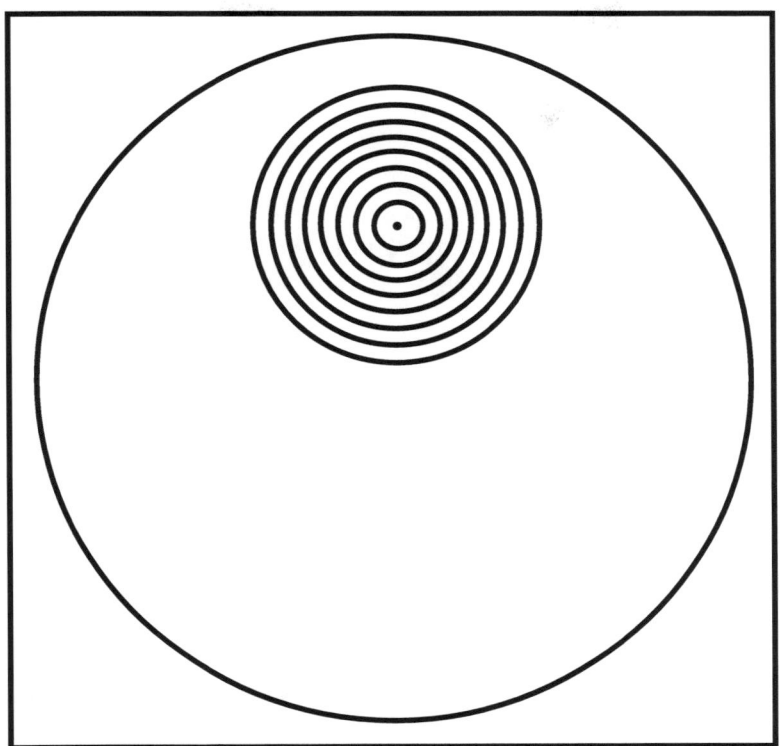

When that one thing
vibrates in particular patterns,
it appears to be something different
than the space in which it is vibrating.

But that is just an appearance.

We know that the rippling water in the pond
has not somehow become something
other than water.

But when the ripple is us and our attention
becomes fixated on our experience of vibration,
we tend to forget our "pondness."

71

Musings:

The questions:
What's wrong with "me?"

Aside from the fact that the separate "me" is an illusion, the problem is not that there is an identity that we call "me." Rather, the problem is that we identify so exclusively with that identity that we do not recognize it as an identity or a story. Instead it <u>is</u> us. It is not just our story. It becomes the truth of who and what we are. And because that truth appears separate and needs to appear separate to justify its existence, we end up cut off from the oneness that is the actual truth of our existence—the very thing for which we are searching. We feel this separation as an anxious sense that "this" and "now" is never enough.

We are longing to return home—to dissolve into the one ocean from which we all arise as GOD playing with GOD. But, because we can only see separate forms and we believe in the fundamental separateness of our own form, the only answer to that anxious longing is seeking. Since "this" and "now"—what is arising right here in this moment—is never enough to overcome the empty pain of separation, we become seekers.

We are trying to fill a hole. We fill it with possessions, but possessions can be taken away or we can lose interest in them. We fill it with relationships, but relationships change and relationships end. We fill it with spiritual pursuits, but even those don't fully pierce the veil that keeps us from seeing the truth. We fill it with things that are, by their very nature, impermanent and transient. The happiness of the separate "me" ends up depending upon things that do not last, which keeps us locked in a cycle of seeking and cursed with having our attention always directed at some moment other than here and now.

There is nothing wrong with "me" except that "me" is an illusion that keeps us locked in suffering.

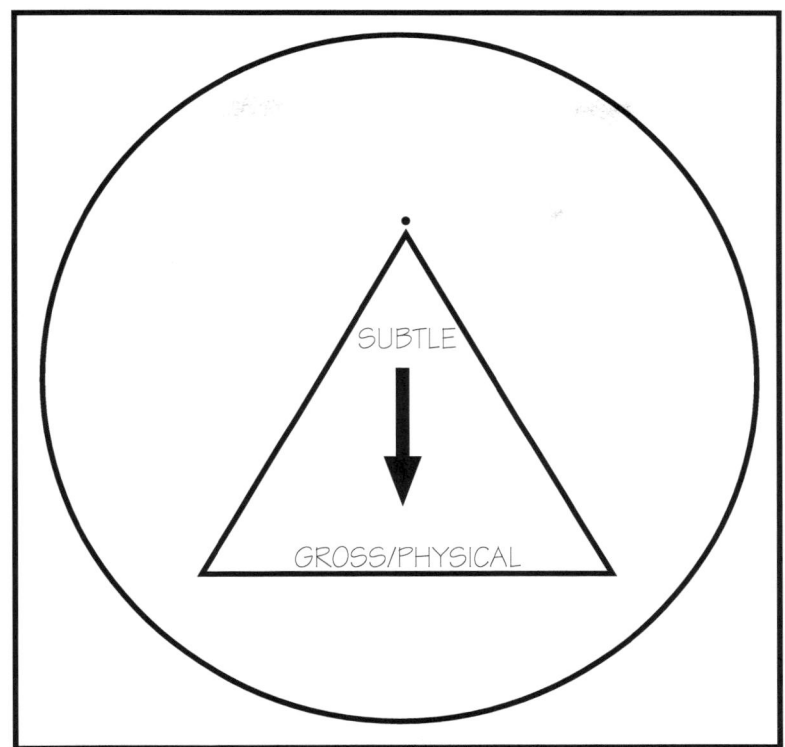

But let's go back to that first drop.
It creates a vibration
in the ocean of consciousness.
From that first vibration, form manifests.

And it seems to manifest
from the subtle to the gross,
from the lightest to the most dense.

There are many levels of subtlety before arriving at
the body we call mental or mind.

Musings:

 The questions:
Does the "me" go away?

Yes and no. The "me" is an illusion and, once we really become aware of that fact, it is hard to willingly embrace it as a fact the way we once did, so its influence over us tends to fade or dissolve.

There is also a "me" that lingers. That "me" sometimes returns as habitual patterns. Even people who have had profound experiences of awakening sometimes find that a "me" wants to reassert itself. They may be absolute poster children for nonduality in most of the aspects of their lives and yet still constrict around an old identity, a "me," when it comes to some area of life like relationship or money.

It is also true that if one is going to move among people for whom the myth of their identity is still "the truth," it can be helpful to have a "me" costume to slip on when appropriate. In fact people who have had profound awakenings tend to appear in the world in one of three ways.

They may appear to be highly energized with the light of consciousness radiating out from them. They will affect people by their very presence and seem very charismatic, without being manipulative or needing to control anything. It will seem to others as if there is a very radiant "me" emanating from them.

They may also be what I might describe as translucent or transparent. It might feel to others as if there is a "me" there but at the same time not there—present in an enigmatic way that is hard to describe, a shimmer or shadow cast by nothing.

Finally, there may seem to be a multitude of lightly held "me's" emanating from the person. Having made the commitment to serve love and consciousness by "wave-ing" in GODs ocean, a variety of playful "me" identities might be useful.

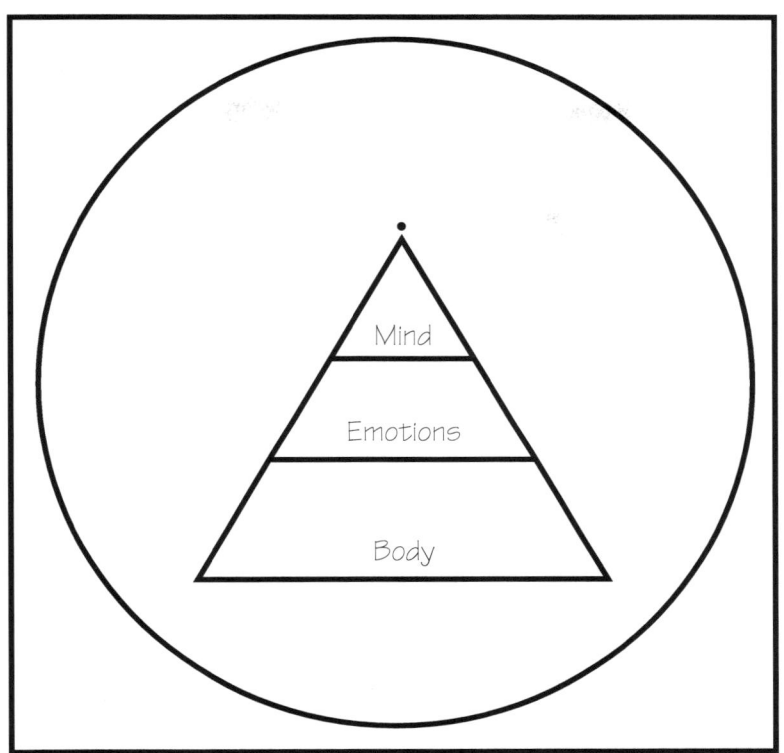

Many traditions identify
a plethora of subtle bodies
prior to the mental body,
but to keep things simple
(and in alignment with our previous model)
we will place the mental body, or mind,
at the top of our pyramid.

As subtle energies coalesce we call them mind.
Mind coagulates into emotion,
and as emotional energy becomes more dense,
we call it the physical body.

Musings:

 The questions:
What will happen to my preferences?

One of the myths of enlightenment is that it means not caring about anything. This arises again from "the world is perfect as it is" notion. Caring about things arises from having preferences and preferences become embedded in and reinforce identities, "I like _____, therefore I am."

When I go to a theater to watch a film and I'm sitting in the dark with a screen and a sound system that nearly fills my perceptual capacity and the movie is well-made and compelling, I become absorbed in the story. In that moment, I believe in the reality of the world I'm watching unfold. I cry or laugh. I'm startled. I'm uplifted or saddened. I experience preferences arising. I want the hero to win. I don't want this character to die or to suffer. I want him to end up with her. I want a happy ending. I may feel disappointment if my preferences aren't met. I may feel sadness if the hero dies or if the lovers cannot be together, but when I leave the movie, especially a well-conceived, believably-acted, and artfully-constructed movie, I feel the perfection in the story. Despite my preferences, the world of the film is perfect as it is. I am grateful to have experienced it and now it is over and something else is arising.

In life, most of what causes suffering is that we have these preferences that we believe define who we are as separate beings. Those preferences are usually a desire for external circumstances—things we cannot control—to be different than they are. We spend a lot of time and energy trying to control those circumstances and satisfy our preferences. It is logical to believe that if we had no preferences, we would no longer suffer. We may try to exert control over some of our preferences, like an addict avoiding an addictive behavior, but that is not enlightenment.

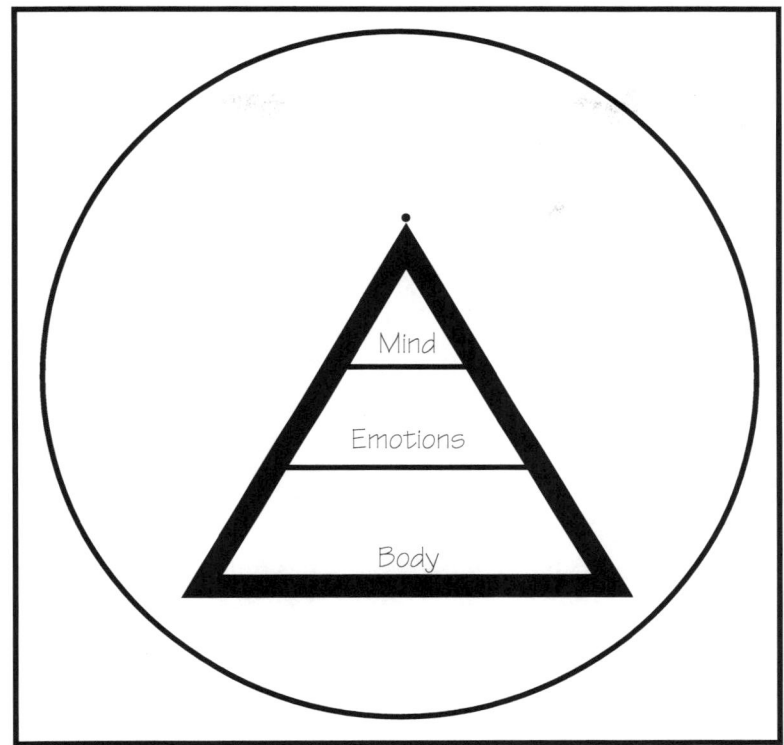

The awareness of these
realms of perceptual experience
that arise from the space of pure consciousness
begins to create a personality or an ego
that feels pretty solid and separate,
because it is based on identification
with the vibratory nature or aspect
of consciousness, usually at the expense
of identification with the space of consciousness.

We forget who we really are in order to
play the game of form.

Musings:

The questions:
How does nonduality relate to
enlightenment?

In order to awaken from the dream of separation and realize the truth, we need to recognize the false nature of duality.

Einstein said that GOD created time so that everything wouldn't happen all at once. It might be more accurate to say that the dual mind created time for that reason. After all, why would GOD have a problem with everything happening all at once?

That is how experience happens, all at once in one place—now. The first function of the dual mind (the top layer, as it were) is to extract aspects of the now that are arising and name them. That's a table. That's a wine glass. That's a loaf of bread. That's a woman smiling at me as she touches her hair. As we name them, we create the things that are me and the things that are not me. The moment we name them, we no longer have to really look at them, in effect we stop really seeing them and insert a mental or conceptual placeholder for them.

If we peel back the layer of naming, which is something <u>we</u> do to experience (a chair does not know itself to be a chair) rather than something that is inherent in the experience itself, then we are left with the next layer, which is perceiving. But does any sensation/vibration/perception exist beyond the act or apparatus of perceiving? It is hard to imagine an example.

So naming and perceiving are overlays we place on experience. They can and do only occur within us. That leaves us with a confusing term that is often called the such-ness or is-ness of an experience.

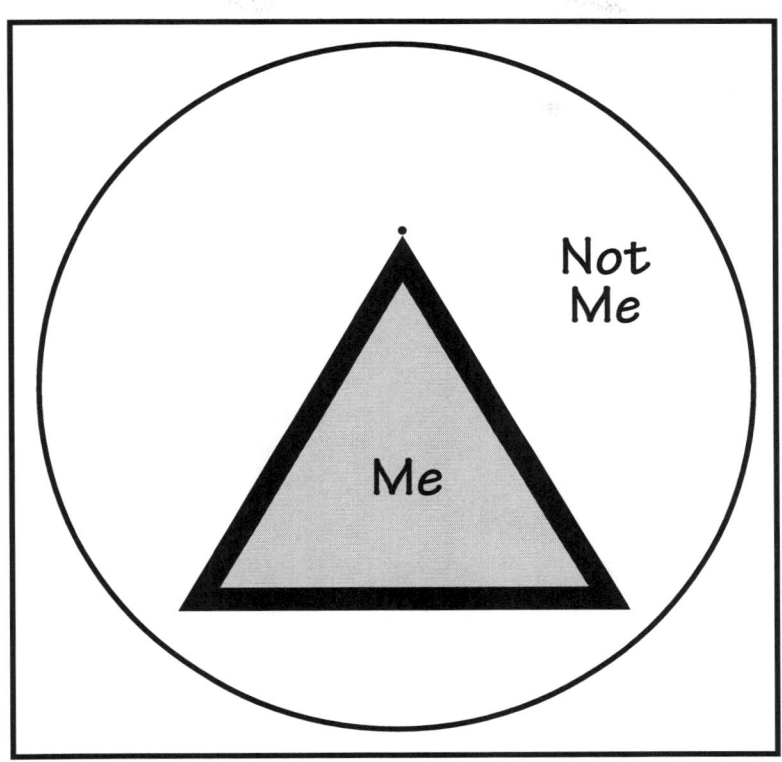

We create a personality structure that separates us
from the space of consciousness which is our true
nature and the true nature of all form.

We see separation rather than unity.
We think we are our thoughts,
our emotions, and our bodies.

Musings:

 The questions:
Such-ness and is-ness?

The such-ness or is-ness of an object or phenomena is both its quality of being and the experience we have of knowing that being arising at the same moment as "not two" (advaita) but one simultaneous experience. This is consciousness recognizing itself as consciousness.

Aside from the labels we give to things and the qualities we perceive in things, the dual mind tends to think that things (forms) exist separate of our knowing them. They exist in an abstract and conceptual point in the future (not now) waiting for us to encounter them. But we never do encounter them in the future. If we encounter them at all, we encounter them in the now, in the present moment. It may be that things do exist separate from our knowing them, but we have no evidence of that being true. We have no proof.

We may have fantasies about the things we do not yet know or have not yet encountered, just as we may seem to have memories of a time when we did not know something or had not yet encountered something, but these fantasies and memories always occur in the present moment.

The dual mind also tends to place the "being" of a thing "over there" and the "knowing" of a thing "over here." But if there is no evidence for the "being" of a thing without the "knowing" of a thing and no evidence for the "knowing" of a thing without the "being" of a thing, how can they be two things separated by space? When "being" recognizes itself in "knowing" and "knowing" recognizes itself in "being," there are no longer two things, only one.

And if there is only one thing, there is nothing left to seek.

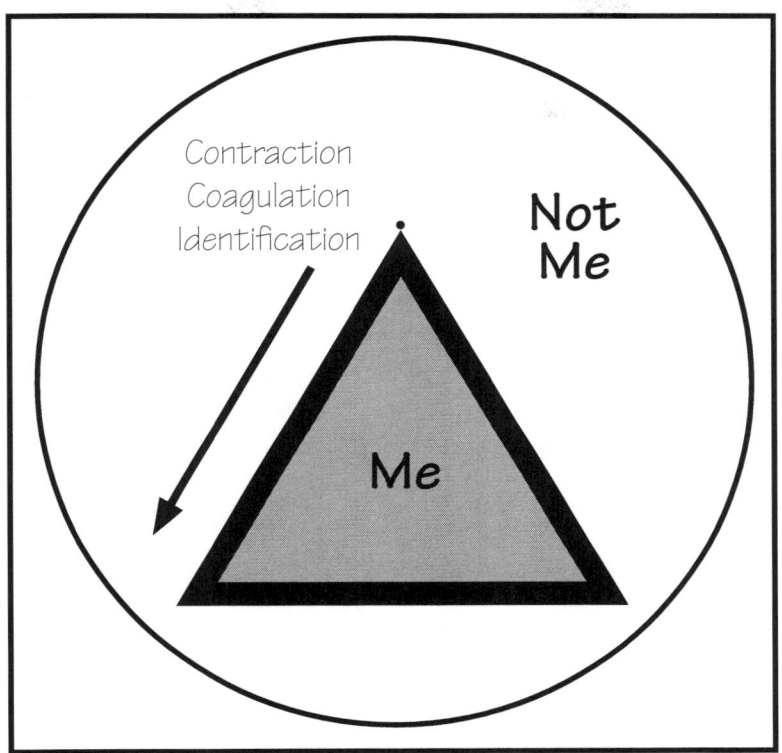

This process is a contraction.

GOD contracts from a spaciousness to a point.
GOD coagulates from what has had no form.
GOD forgets GOD and an "I" is born.
"I" identify with vibration.

I develop a healthy, functioning ego
which means I adopt a workable lie.

It's a lie, but it's a good lie,
like "no that dress doesn't make you look fat,"
or "it's fine that we're just friends."

Musings:

The questions:
What is enlightenment?

Enlightenment is what happens when consciousness recognizes itself.

When this happens, we simply stop seeking. We stop looking outside of ourselves for the objects or conditions that we once thought would bring us peace and contentment if we actually had them. We realize that peace and contentment, the filling of that empty space of longing, the return home to oneness, only really occurs when we stop seeking.

Seeking is the act of objectifying and projecting what is actually us onto something that we imagine to be not us and not here and not now.

Everything we seek and cannot find either compels us to keep searching or drags us into depression and depletes the vitality and aliveness from the present moment. And everything that we seek and find is impermanent. It satisfies us just enough to maintain the illusion that the next thing we seek and find will truly make us happy and will truly be permanent.

Enlightenment is when, despite all our resistance and procrastination, GOD grabs us by the scruff of the neck and makes us look into that clear, still reflecting pool and see the truth of what we really are. This doesn't take practice as much as a letting go.

We can spend years distracting ourselves and actively avoiding GOD's reflecting pool. We can even more subtly avoid GOD by spending years "seeking" GOD. But in the end, when we are ready, or when GOD is ready for us, it only takes an instant.

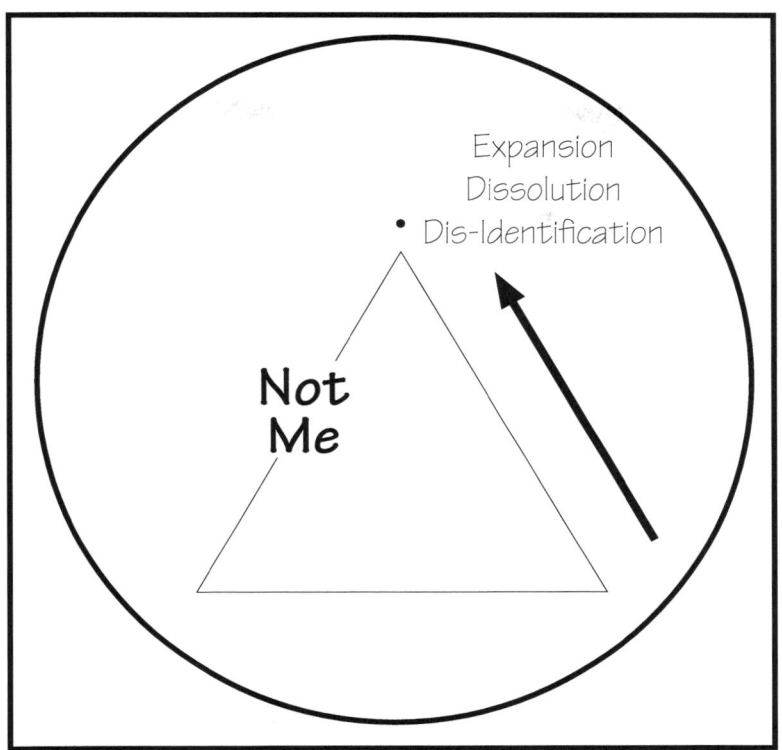

Its counterpart is expansion.

The "I" that I thought I was (actually GOD)
expands into the subtle space of consciousness.
What has become stuck, dissolves.
I (GOD as me) dis-identify with the personality
and the transitory nature of the
vibratory experience.

I stop believing in "the" lie and develop a
distaste for all lies.

Since most, if not all, of our relationships are based
on "the good lies," this can be a difficult process.

83

Musings:

 The questions:
Would I know if I was enlightened?

Only if you pay the $49.95 for the framed certificate.

The traditional answer is that it would require a perceiving identity, a "me," to know whether I had achieved enlightenment, but enlightenment is supposedly the death of the "me" that would be able to identify the desired or anticipated state of enlightenment.

There are, I'm sure, very clever answers for this question, but at a more practical level, we can say that from this side of enlightenment, it is often seen as a dividing line and a goal. "She's enlightened and he's not." "If only I could..., then I'd be enlightened." It becomes just another goal for a spiritual seeker. Just another identity.

From the other side of enlightenment, however, it is simply the truth. It is obvious and self-evident and claiming it as an identity seems rather silly. It is as if we were all searching for air (without really knowing what air is). Whole religions could be built around masters who had become "enbreathened" and were now actually breathing air. Once one actually became "enbreathened," however, one would realize that breathing air is not a special gift. It is the truth of existence. It is what everyone does.

From another purely practical perspective it can get confusing to the rest of us when someone is describing in great detail the many experiential changes in perception and understanding he or she experienced upon waking up, while at the same time saying there is no separate identity left within them capable of identifying whether they are enlightened or not.

At the very least, there seems to be enough of a "me" left to identify the profound shifts in awareness they have experienced.

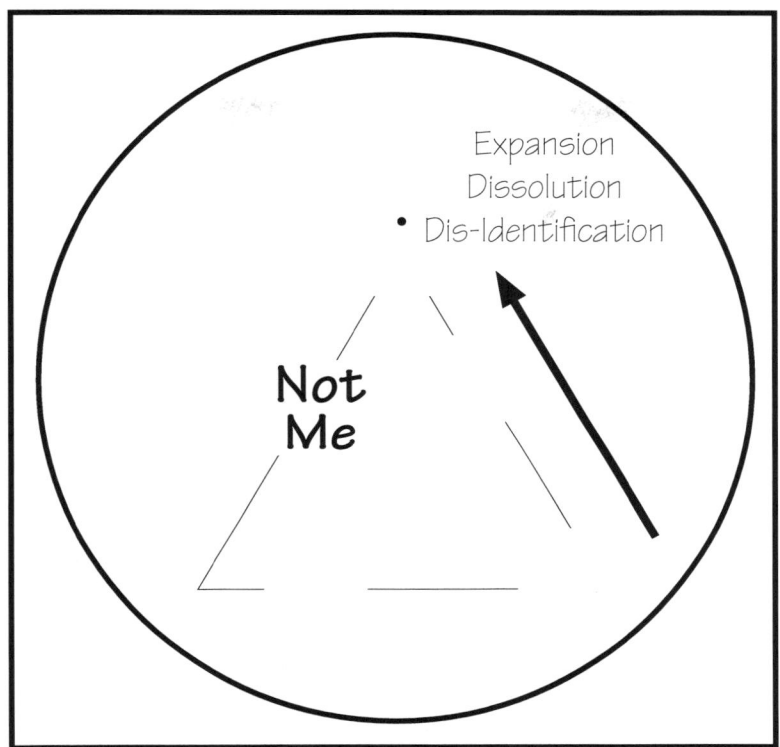

In this dissolution,
our egos become transparent or more flexible.

We experience unity more than separation.

We experience non-attachment.

Don't get confused by the apparent contraction from a wide base to a narrow apex in this upward gesture. This movement actually expands what is me from a fixed form to an expansive space by dissolving the boundaries of form.

Musings:

 The questions:
Then what causes enlightenment?

A $10,000 spiritual retreat, plus the $49.95 for the framed certificate.

The truth is that no one knows for sure. Some religions or philosophies or belief systems seem to map out a direct route built out of some combination of spiritual practices, energetic shock therapy and/or direct contact with enlightened beings. One does not need to look far to find teachers offering to confer enlightenment through kundalini awakening experiences or other such energetic methods, though whether this is anything more than a series of state of consciousness changes masquerading as a stage of evolutionary growth change, is unclear. Traditions like Vedanta emphasize knowledge as the path to enlightenment. Other belief systems claim there is no path to enlightenment, because any path would require doing and desire, which are anathema to pure awareness.

Some people seem to find it in tradition-rich spiritual communities and other people find it alone on park benches or apartments in crowded cities. On the solitary path, those who awaken seem to experience profound suffering and dysfunction on the way to enlightenment. Mental illness, depression, profound existential dissatisfaction and even thoughts of suicide are not uncommon in those circling close to enlightenment.

There is also some common ground in that those who experience enlightenment have usually done some kind of deep introspection, usually supported by meditation, direct inquiry, religious or spiritual study, intense journaling or the contemplation of what are called "pointing out instructions." Some people do all of these things and don't wake up and, reportedly, some people do none of these things and do wake up.

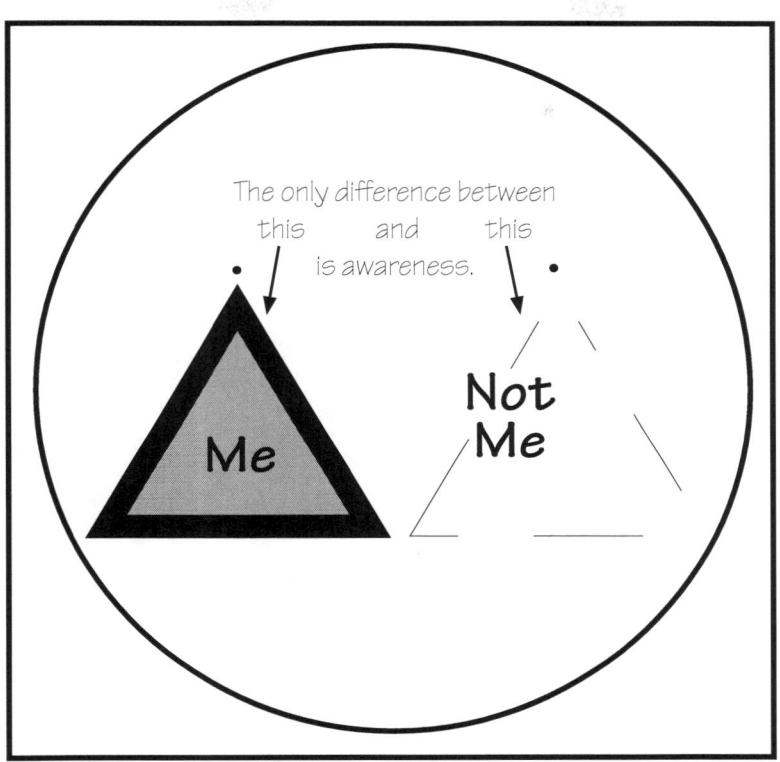

One could wake up from the sleep
that is identification with form
at any moment,
by simply waking up.

It is also true that there are various exercises
and practices that can bring
awareness into the experience of the vibratory
realm of form.

One of the most powerful is stillness.
In stillness, what is "here" and "now" is enough.

Musings:

 The questions:
How does meditation help?

Meditation helps you develop stillness, unyoke attention from thought, and develop witness consciousness. The point of meditation is not to stop thoughts or create some system for screening out thoughts you don't like. The point is to return to a proper relationship to those thoughts. They are not who you are.

Imagine watching a movie screen upon which little snippets of images from different films appear. You might see a painful moment of betrayal in love, followed by an embarrassing moment of humiliation in a child's life, followed by the breathtaking beauty of a mountain sunset, followed by a violent attack on one person by another, followed by a moment of delicious intimacy, followed by a dark erotic fantasy, followed by an image of a man accomplishing a mission he has struggled all his life to complete.

The more real these images seem and the more emotionally entangled we become in what we are seeing, the more we identify with what we are seeing. We believe that screen is us. It is who we are. Those things are happening to a "me." We have feelings about it and those feelings reinforce the connection to the images.

Meditation is a process for placing yourself back in the audience, remembering that all of these images are being generated and projected onto a screen that happens to be your mind. If you get lost in them, you suffer. If you remember that these thoughts are not who you are, you may still experience the flow of feeling—pain and pleasure, but they are not you and they do not linger. They simply move on.

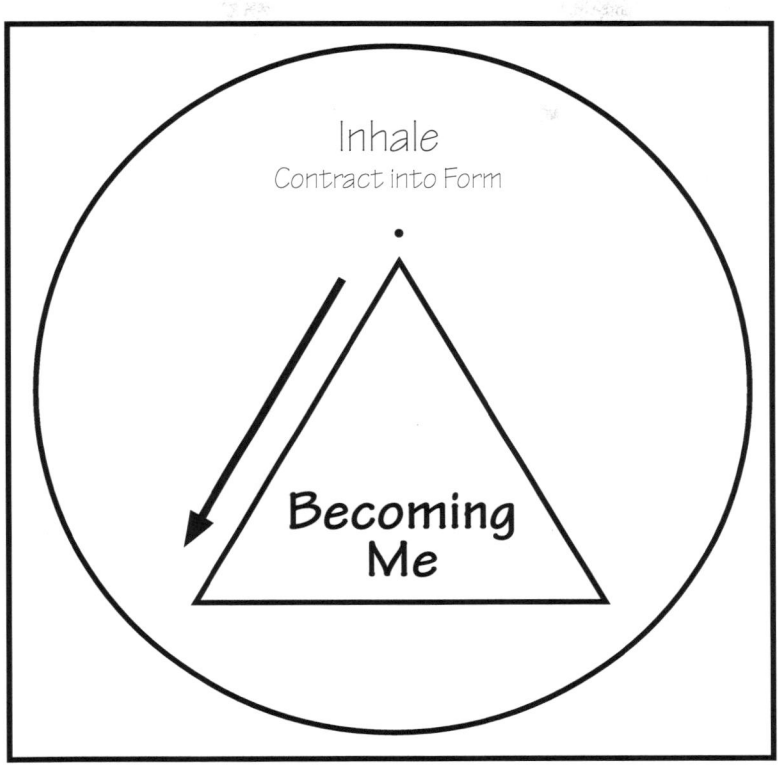

In stillness, we bring awareness to mind, emotion,
and body without identifying with it.
We recognize form as GOD (core consciousness)
vibrating in a certain pattern.

From this perspective, there is no wrong move.

It's a game that can be enthusiastically
and passionately played.
GOD inhales and contracts to dance or wrestle
with other forms.

We become the wave.

Musings:

 The questions:
And what about direct inquiry?

People seem to be able to practice meditation for many years without reaching the kind of breakthrough awakening that is described as enlightenment. Meditation produces all sorts of physiological, psycho-emotional, and spiritual benefits of its own, and even if it had no relationship to enlightenment, would be a practice worth cultivating. While meditation may not be <u>the</u> vehicle for enlightenment, it seems to prepare the ground for what is ultimately a very destabilizing event: awakening.

On the other hand, more people claim to have experienced that awakening as a result of some form of self-inquiry or deep, radical questioning of existence and identity. The form of self-inquiry may be teacher-directed and steeped in a tradition like Zen Buddhism or it may be naive (in the sense of being un-trained or not classically schooled) and self-generated.

Direct inquiry is, as it sounds, a direct and unmediated questioning of the very fundamentals of existence: reality, identity, suffering, and transcendence. It seems to be most successful when the stakes are highest. When we reach a point where we just can't go on sleepwalking another minute, when the suffering we create for ourselves is clearly seen and understood, and when the distracting anesthesia of seeking and acquiring wears off enough to feel the formerly dull ache of separation as a gaping wound, the questions of direct inquiry can pull back the veil.

But there is nothing magical about direct inquiry itself. It can be coopted to play intellectual games and dance all around pure awareness without ever crossing the threshold. It's best use seems to be as a kind of sword for cutting through anything that is not absolutely true, and what is left is pure awareness.

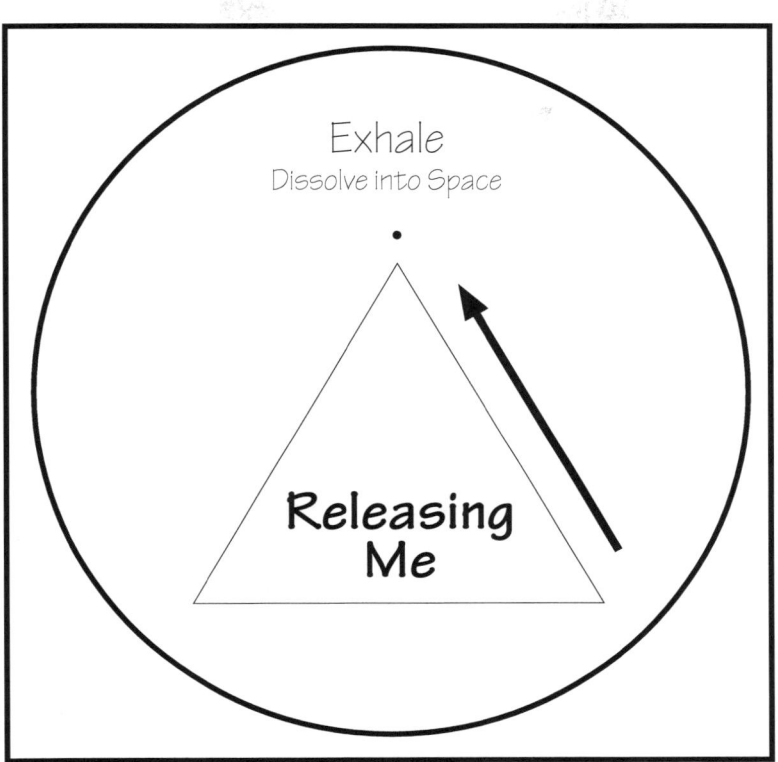

Then the wave dissolves.

We release attachment to form and permanence.
We exhale and relax.

We experience unity and freedom and bliss
as we return to the ocean of consciousness
that is our true nature.

Of course, I'm rather unfairly characterizing this as
being easy. It isn't. It is very hard and can be very
frightening to truly let go of every thing you think
you need and think you are.

Musings:

 The questions:
How do practices correspond to the
cycle of formlessness into form?

*On one side, in the descent of GOD's mysterious contraction
into form, we have developed practices and therapies aimed at
making us more functional forms. As beings heavily identified with form and the vibratory experience, we have the most
practices for the things we care the most about: coupling, com-
munication, manifestation, power, and control.*

*At the base of the triangle diagram, in the space between the
complete identification with form and the recognition of the
emptiness of that identification, we have, at one side, "spiritual
practices" aimed at perfecting our spiritual forms or in some
way liberating us from the purely vibratory experience, such
as meditation for compassion or meditation on form, Tantra
and kundalini awakening, sacred and ecstatic dance, trance,
prayer, devotion, art, chanting, breathwork and the Yogas. As
we approach the other side of the base of the triangle, the practices become, meditation on formlessness, direct inquiry, and
the contemplation of pointing-out instructions.*

*On the side of ascent—GOD's mysterious dissolution of form
and the play of consciousness recognizing itself—we are in the
realm of "no practice," because to practice requires a goal and
a goal requires a seeker and a seeker requires a sense of separation and lack and the sense of separation and lack is what we
release in order exhale and dissolve.*

*None of this is absolute. I am merely describing the appearance
of a tendency.*

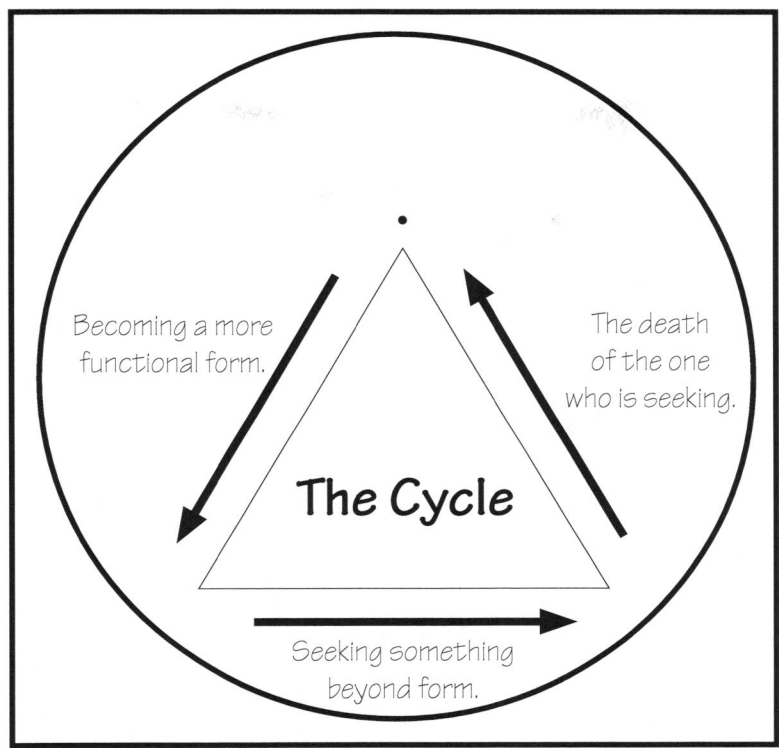

This pulsation
between emptiness and form
is a dialogue of sorts
between the absolute stillness
of consciousness
and the passionate vibration of form.

Musings:

The questions:
What keeps this cycle of contraction
and dissolution from being seamless?

Because we are talking about the relationship between something and nothing, which is very un-non-dual (how's that for a double negative?), I'm going to describe a duality that does seem useful to consider in this particular realm.

We we seem to incarnate in this life with an ascending aspect and a descending aspect. Our ascending or spiritual aspect looks up and out. It thinks in terms of transcending all the pain and unpleasantness of this incarnation. Our descending or soul aspect looks down and in. It thinks in terms of embracing and reveling in all the possible experiences of this realm.

When our descending aspect is dominant, we tend to over-psychologize. We find our pathologies endlessly fascinating and completely identify with our little egoic constrictions. We bind through our wounds and highly value our status as victims. We define ourselves as introverts or extraverts, wounded children, survivors, and archetypes and create elaborate identities based on having our boundaries respected and our identities reinforced.

When our ascending aspect is dominant, we tend to over-spiritualize. We repress our negative feelings as being wrong, bad, or not spiritually elevated. We avoid pain through spiritual bypassing that shows up as escapism ("My life sucks, so I'll just avoid it by taking another spiritual weekend workshop"), idiot compassion ("It's all good!"), over-valuing certain emotions and repressing or devaluing other emotions as not being spiritual enough ("I've done my work and I don't get angry!"), and magical thinking ("If I visualize it strong enough and command it to be so, I will get it.").

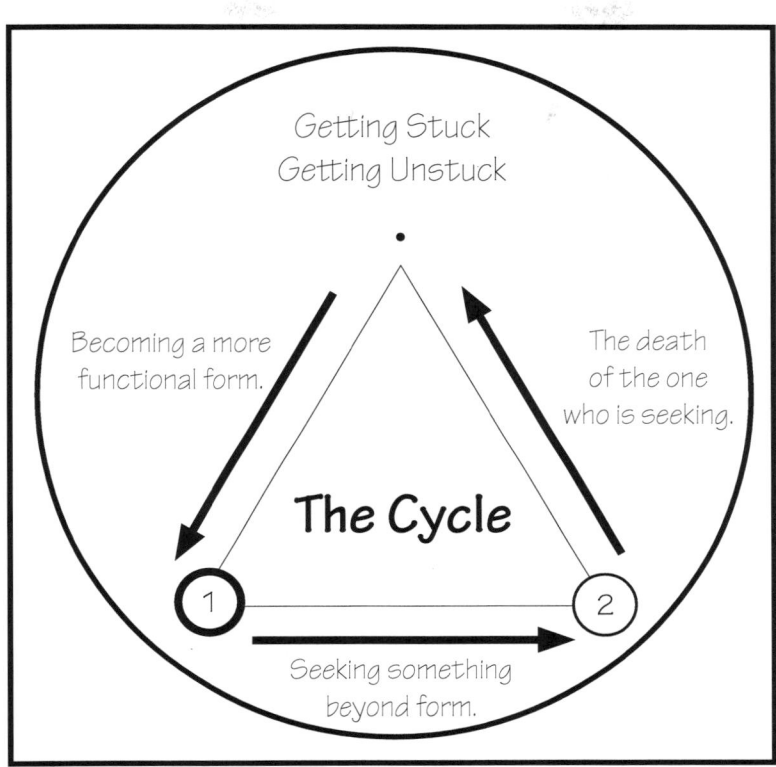

Within this cycle we get stuck in two
fairly common places.

(1). Once we are fully invested in our material
form, we tend to get stuck there.
This is an individual and egoic stuck place as well
as the cultural stuck place of scientific materialism,
which says there is only form and nothing else.

"I spent all this energy becoming me and now you
are telling me that I'm not really me!"

Musings:

 The questions:
How can we see form and formlessness as one phenomenon?

Whether you accept the literal truth of the chakras or not, they are a useful metaphor for the ascending and descending nature of incarnation. The ascending aspect is represented in the energy body as the upper three chakras (crown, third eye, and throat). The descending aspect is represented as the lower three chakras (root, naval, solar plexus). The heart chakra is the balancing or bridge chakra, that should unite the descending (embracing) and ascending (transcendent) impulses into a seamless experience, but it often cannot function because it is so armored. When the heart is armored, one or the other aspect tends to become dominant.

Spiritual bypassing manifests as an avoidance or repression of lower chakra concerns (survival, elimination, the body, sexuality, egoic shadow, addiction, identity, and relationship). Over-psychologizing tends to repress or trivialize the upper chakra concerns of will, creativity, vision, and transcendence.

In balance, we need both the descending impulse and the ascending impulse. The descending impulse is to dive down into and embrace—think Dionysus or Kali. It gives us great art, beauty, passion, and poetry as we consciously and compassionately enter the dreaming world.

The ascending impulse is to ascend and transcend—think Buddha or Kwan Yin. It gives us the clear light of truth and expansive consciousness as we dissolve all illusory boundaries between forms and rest in pure awareness.

We can find in this embodied experience a kind of constant dynamic balance of inhalation and exhalation, constriction and relaxation, something and nothing.

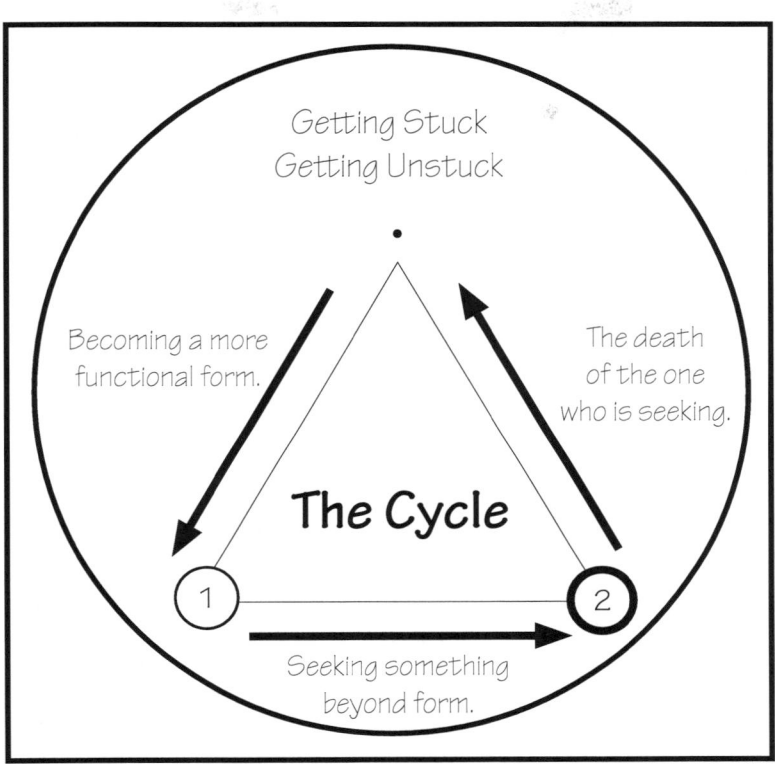

(2). Once we intuit or realize that there is something beyond the material form and its pursuits, we tend to convert our material seeker into a spiritual seeker and pursue a sort of energetic mastery.

There is nothing wrong with this,
but ultimately, we have to
release even the seeker,
and this can lead to the second place
in which we get stuck.
The inability to let go of our attachment
to our spiritual identities.

Musings:

The questions:
And where does this leave us?

I suppose the point for me in all of this is that if awakening from the dream of duality requires that I withdraw from life and relationship and art and beauty and love in order to maintain my wakefulness, then nondual awareness, for me, ends up missing something vital.

It may bring the end of suffering, But at what cost?

We have an overabundance of enlightened role models from the classical tradition who could only deal with their enlightened state and heightened sensitivities by withdrawing from the world or creating insulated communities. Remaining at play in the fields of the lord is usually suspect.

Equanimity and peaceful abiding may be a by-product of the awakened state, but what about compassionate engagement?

The truth of space—consciousness—does not need to negate the arising of vibration and form.

> *"Then the Heart realizes that the true innate nature is both the universal agent and the subjectivity that perceives the world. Thus immersed in understanding, it knows and acts according to its desire."*

> Stanza 10 of *The Yoga Spandakarika*
> translated by Daniel Odier

Now lets see what paradoxes arise when we seek enlightenment.

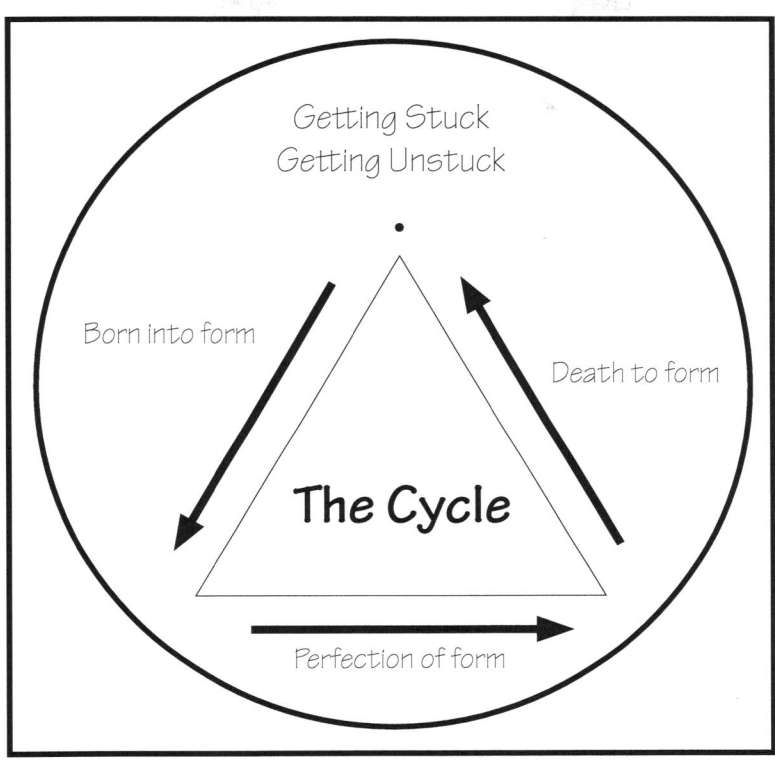

So the relationship between the form that practices
being a more functional form and the form that
develops a high degree of artistry or mastery with
the flow of energy and the form that awakens from
the dream of separateness, can be a natural and
cyclical one.

As long as the cycle continues
and does not bind at any one point
by clinging to a fixed identity or form,
there need not be a conflict between
the duality of appearance
and the reality of oneness.

Chapter Four
Seeking Enlightenment

First there is a mountain.
Then there is no mountain.
Then there is.

Musings:

 Pre-thought

When an infant gazes up at us in awe and wonder, we smile. We can't help it.

An infant is in a pre-thought, pre-conceptual, state. The only time it knows is now. It seems as if it recognizes itself in us, as if there is no separation between it and us. It encounters us with the same awe and wonder and curiosity that it finds in its own toes and fingers. There is no judgment of us, just as there is no judgment of its own toes and fingers.

Our response to the way we are seen by infants is usually one of joy, because, when faced with this level of loving acceptance, we recognize ourselves in the other, just as we are being recognized.

When we do not experience this sense of joy, it is usually because our sense of self is so clouded and constricted around a particular identity story, that we are unable to feel anything that threatens the story of ourselves as unique and separate beings.

The mystery.
The mystery.
The mystery.

Then I am born.
I incarnate.

The dream begins.

Musings:

 Thought

As beautiful as pre-thought might be in an infant, and as much as it reflects a kind of "natural state," the goal is not to return to and live in a pre-thought state. First of all, that would be impossible. We cannot unlearn. We cannot really regress consciousness.

Contemporary philosopher Ken Wilber has popularized what he calls the pre/trans fallacy. That is what we do when we find the rational state unacceptable or unfulfilling or incomplete. We look backward with regressive fondness to pre-rational states (tribal paradigms, romanticizing indigenous culture, embracing incomplete mythologies). While completely understandable, this embrace of the pre-rational has to bypass or repress the rational. This never works in any lasting way unless we settle for half-truths and compromises.

The goal is to expand and embrace the rational to find the trans-rational or transcendent states. The goal is not to return to some romantic ideal of pre-thought but to expand our consciousness to embrace post-thought—to move through and beyond thought, so that thought can be seen as a tool that can be picked up and set down, rather than as the ground and moderator of all experience.

The pre/trans fallacy also describes what happens when someone in a rational stage of development sees an example of something transcendent or trans-rational and labels it pre-rational, because it is the only description that fits their still-limited model of reality.

I am happy.
I don't need much.
I love everyone.
I am part of everything that is.

I begin to figure out how things work here.

Musings:

 Separation and the seeker

For some reason, we are not born into this realm to remain in a pre-thought stage. Thought probably enabled us to survive and thrive as a species when we were not physiologically as well adapted for our environments.

But along with thought came the primary illusion: separation. And, once you have separation, you have a seeker. We seek because seeking is rooted in the rejection of what is. Because we feel separate, we feel incomplete, and because we feel incomplete, we seek what we believe will complete us.

Usually the things we seek to complete us take the form of relationships, material possessions, security, stability, and power. Much of the indoctrination and enculturation of youth is aimed at ritualizing and codifying and making this socially sanctioned seeking seem normal and healthy.

It is odd that this generally accepted state of seeking, which seems to be reinforced by family and culture destabilizes in two distinct ways. Constantly seeking more in the material realm threatens the environment and produces social schism, inequity, war and aggression. When seeking is turned inward it threatens the very patterns upon which cultural and social order is maintained.

I begin to realize that I am incomplete.

I am supported in this realization
because it is what everyone I know
seems to believe.

I need things to make me happy.
I need people to make me feel whole.

My happiness and my contentment
reside outside of me.

How can I simply be here now?

Musings:

 Seeking is suffering

Siddhārtha Gautama, the Buddha, was a Hindu sage in the same way that Jesus of Nazareth, the Christ, was a Jewish Rabbi. Both were driven by a desire to end suffering and reveal the hidden truth of existence. The Buddha built upon the truths of his day found in the Vedantic (Vedantic means way of knowledge or knowing) tradition.

The Vedantic tradition of Hinduism held that there were five causes of suffering:
- *Not understanding the true nature of reality*
- *Attachment or clinging to transient phenomena*
- *Fear or repulsion of transient phenomena*
- *A false sense of identity*
- *Fear of death*

Of course, they also said that the last four causes could be summed up in the first cause. When we do not understand the true nature of reality, we behave in ways that lead to suffering. And the true nature of reality is that everything that can be perceived is transient and impermanent and illusory.

The Buddha reduced suffering down to one cause. Duhkha, or suffering, was caused by the thirst for (craving or seeking after) things that were, by their very nature, impermanent. If our happiness is dependent upon things that are impermanent, our happiness is destined to be impermanent.

In fact, this Buddha character had a lot to say about suffering and seeking and enlightenment.

There seems to be a mountain.
I think I will find my happiness by climbing it.

The mountain is possessions.
The mountain is wealth.
The mountain is relationships.
The mountain is status.
The mountain is romantic love.

The mountain that seems to be there
is also the me that seems to be here
finding out who I am and who I am not.

But I quickly forget this.

Musings:

 Pain and Suffering

It is important to remember that pain and pleasure are phenomena of this realm of incarnation. We cannot escape them. Trying to escape pain or pleasure is not the same as ending suffering. It, in fact, causes more suffering.

Pain and pleasure are temporary and fleeting experiences. When we dwell upon the pain of the past (the recollected self) or armor ourselves against the pain of an imagined future (the anticipated self), we create suffering. When we lament the fact that we are no longer experiencing a certain pleasure or live in anticipation of a pleasure yet to come, or when our focus in the moment becomes an opportunity for judging and evaluating what is arising as if we were providing play-by-play commentary upon our own existence, we miss the beauty of this moment and create suffering.

Pain is the experience we have. Suffering is the commentary we write in the aftermath of the experience.

I sometimes meditate with my dog. She is a German Shepherd named Maya. Actually, between the two of us, I am the only one capable of holding the concept that we are meditating. I am much better at turning my attention inward past the phenomena of thought to abide with that which is observing. She is much better at experiencing each moment as it arises.

She does not add unnecessary suffering to her day. If I accidently step on her paw, she barks, whines, and limps only as long as she needs to and then opens as love to me almost instantly. If my beloved, accidently hurts my feelings, I generally suppress my barking, whining and limping in such a way that it can be days before I realize how closed my heart has been and how much suffering I've added to a moment of pain.

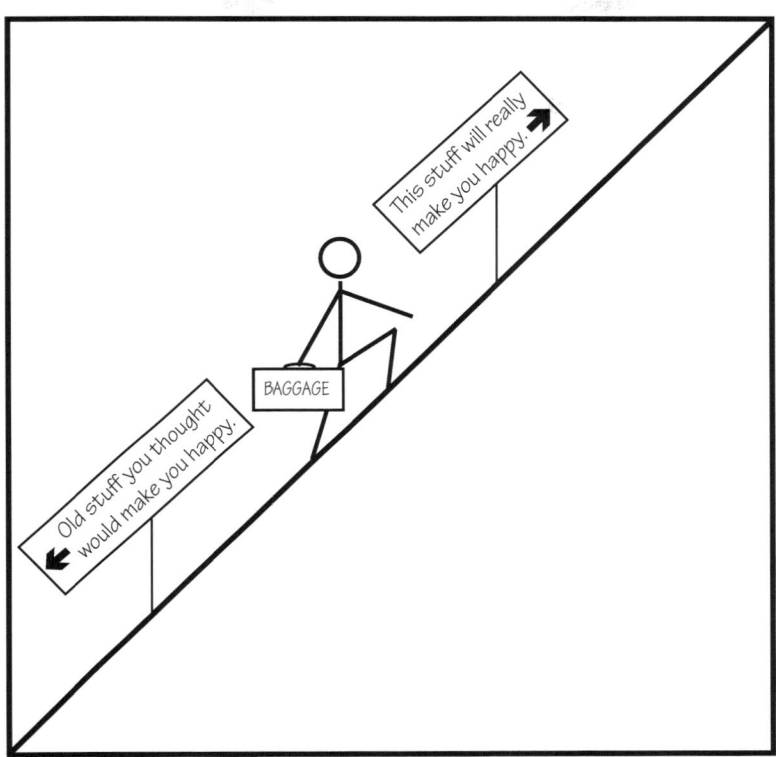

And, sure enough, I find what I am looking for.

I find stuff and relationships that make me happy,
for awhile.

But then I realize I am not really happy, or at least
not as happy as I think I could be.

So I keep some of the stuff,
because I remember how happy it once made me,
and I keep climbing.

Musings:

 Seeking refuge in the sangha

The Buddha said that we may take refuge from suffering in the Buddha, The Dharma and the Sangha.

Said another way, we may take refuge from the storm of suffering that this life appears to be in the idea that someone (the Buddha, or Buddhas, or enlightened beings) found a way to get off the wheel of suffering.

We may also take refuge in the fact that those beings did not simply get off the wheel of suffering. They left a clear path called the Dharma (teachings, instructions, a map) which we may follow.

Finally, we may take refuge in the idea that we are not alone in our desire to end suffering. There is a Sangha (a spiritual community) dedicated to finding an end to suffering and that community can offer us support and strength when challenges arise and our desire fades.

It seems to be in our genetic programming as humans to seek community (for safety, identity, acknowledgement, acceptance), while at the same time, our cultural programing as urban, western, scientific materialists born into the baby boomer-plus generation causes us to distrust community. What that means is that we have an odd and ambivalent relationship to the idea of community. We want to lose ourselves in it and are afraid of becoming lost in it.

We sometimes find ourselves attracted to communities for what they can do for us rather than for how we might serve them. We tend to want to control our communities or our experience of our communities, which leads to...

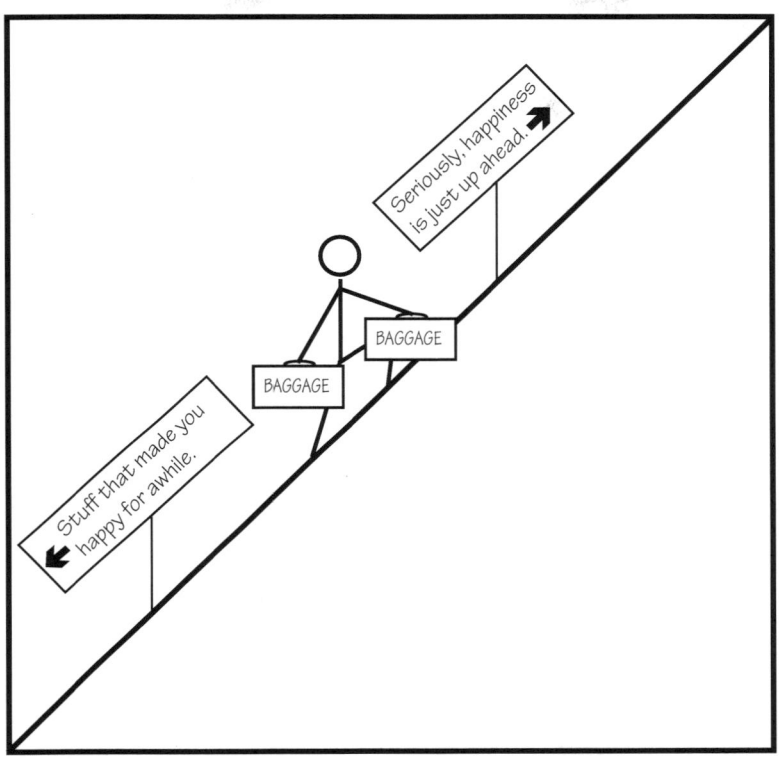

This happens over and over again
but I never question the process itself.

As long as I believe
that there is a me that is separate
from everyone and everything else,
it makes sense that I should keep climbing.

But it does get harder to climb,
harder to reach true happiness,
with all this baggage I'm carrying.

Musings:

 Helping me grow or holding me back?

...the dangers of the sangha.

We can intellectually understand what nondual awareness means and still not let that meaning penetrate our core. But, regardless of how deeply we live that truth, we also live in a world of apparent duality. In that world of apparent distinction, we may at any moment, perceive others to be more or less sensitive or aware or conscious than ourselves. We may also feel drawn to people who seem to be more aware and conscious and sensitive. In some ways, surrounding ourselves with other sensitive and aware and conscious beings can support us on our spiritual path, but there are two potential problems.

The first problem is how we relate to the members of our community. If we have invested a lot of energy in the idea that these people are more sensitive and aware than other people (and how positive we feel to be included in such a group), we are living a delusion. How many times have we been drawn to communities or groups that seemed to be more sensitive and aware, but who, in many ways or at least in specific areas were as insensitive or unaware as anyone else? If we are attached to "our tribe" being a certain way, we either have to deny the truth of what we observe or face the possibility of disappointment or betrayal.

The second problem is that what we are often drawn to in others are those things that reinforce our own ego identities. Am I drawn to them because of their sensitivity or because they validate my sensitivity? Am I drawn to this group because they are so like me or because I want to see myself as being like them?

It can get very confusing.

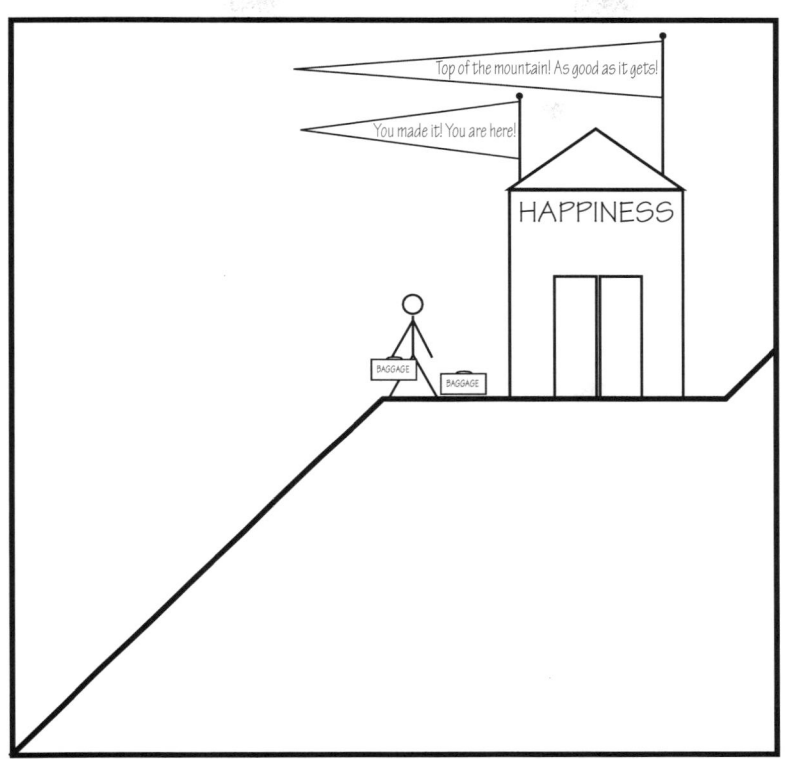

Sometimes, though,
it feels like I've actually made it.
The perfect house.
The perfect job.
The perfect romantic soulmate.
The perfect family.

I'm not alone here.
There are lots of people here with me.
It gives me that sense of who I am
that I have been looking for.

Life is good...

Musings:

 If we are all one,
why do people seem so different?

Oneness doesn't mean sameness. Because I recognize an underlying unity does not mean that every wave that rises up is the same identical wave. Each wave appears different.

Some waves lap gently at a shoreline. Other waves overwhelm a coast and crush everything in their path. It seems like we spend the first part of our lives trying to identify and define just what kind of wave we are. We find waves that are similar to us and that becomes reassuring.

Probably most people are content to live and die just knowing what kind of wave they are, but some people, for whatever reason, begin to see the ocean-ness in the waves rather than just the wave-ness. This doesn't make them better and it doesn't mean they are any less the unique wave they appear to be. It does mean that they take wave-ness (and all the egoic separation that goes with it) less and less seriously.

In fact, as much the advocates of nonduality like to talk about the end of the "self" or the "me" or the unique identity, a world without the appearance of those unique identities would be pretty bland.

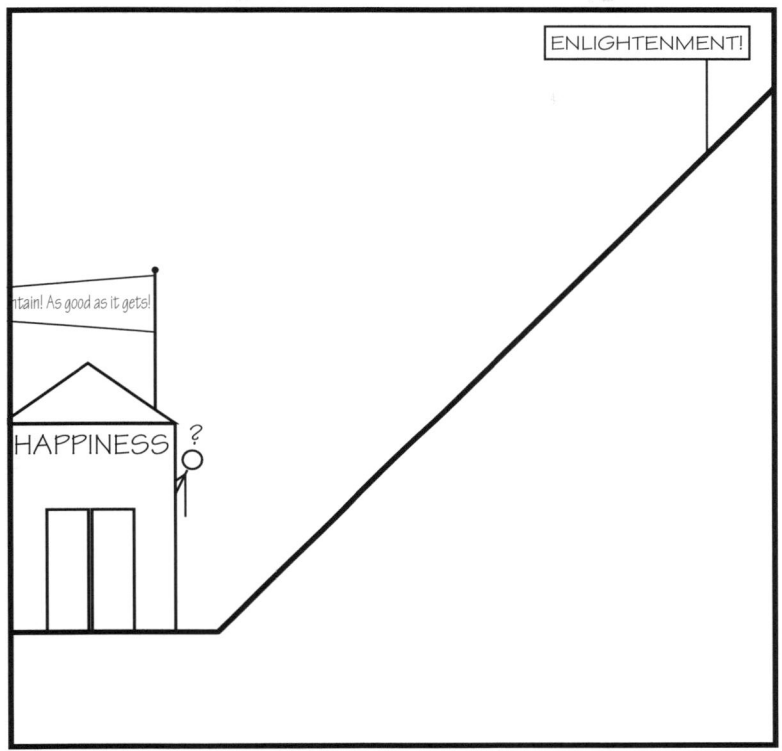

...until it isn't.

Sometimes there is a crisis.
Sometimes there is a dark night of the soul.
Sometimes there is an illness.
Sometimes there is a wrenching away
of my identity.

And sometimes
there is just an itch—an intuition—a sense
that this is not all there is.

Musings:

 ## The eternal ego battle

I used to believe that I was the problem. It seemed very logical and rational. I was my ego and my ego was the problem. It was my ego that needed to go.

I used to growl at mirrors, because that same old guy I saw over and over again was messing up my plans. If I could only look in the mirror and see someone different, I would finally be happy.

I used to believe that I needed to wrestle my ego to the ground in defeat. I needed to drag my defeated ego behind my chariot as I circled the city of Troy three times.

But who is the "me" that needs to defeat my ego?

Another ego!

It is not possible for an ego to get rid of an ego and the egolessness that underlies ego does not need to get rid of ego.

The ocean does not try to get rid of the waves.

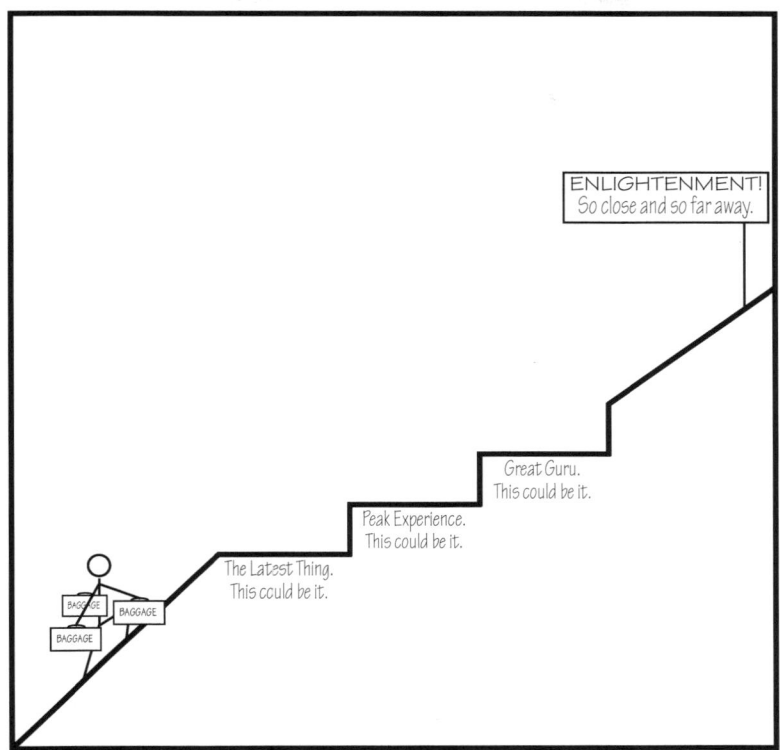

So I pack my bags
and head up the mountain on a spiritual quest.

There are many paths toward enlightenment,
which I am now calling ultimate happiness.

There are also many distractions.
The siren song of the "happy" people down below
makes me question myself.

Did I mention how hard it was
to climb with all this baggage?

Musings:

 The relationship of spiritual practice to awakening

There are spiritual practices and then there is awakening and the relationship between the two is tenuous.

To practice something, you need to perceive a state or stage that is not currently you, but which you might attain. Spiritual practice can give you glimpses of the awakened state but probably won't take you to an awakened stage—an abiding with the true nature of reality.

When you are awake, you don't practice sleeping—you go to sleep. You may hover for a moment in the space between waking and sleeping, but you're not practicing anything, you are either asleep or awake.

When you are asleep, you don't practice waking up—you wake up! Again, you may feel half-awake, but you are not practicing wakefulness, you are either awake or asleep.

There are many beautiful practices for developing spiritual qualities like devotion, equanimity, compassion, and mindfulness, all important qualities in their own right. But many spiritual practices are more likely to reinforce a spiritual identity then to lead to an abiding awareness of the true nature of reality. This new "spiritual" identity may be a superior identity in terms of ultimate functionality, but it is not the same as being awakened.

But, having said all that, there are a handful of spiritual practices that do seem to move one more consistently <u>toward</u> nondual awareness. There are practices that help us become lucid dreamers. There are also practices that help us wake up from our waking dream. These practices use meditation and inquiry to pierce the veil between what appears and what is.

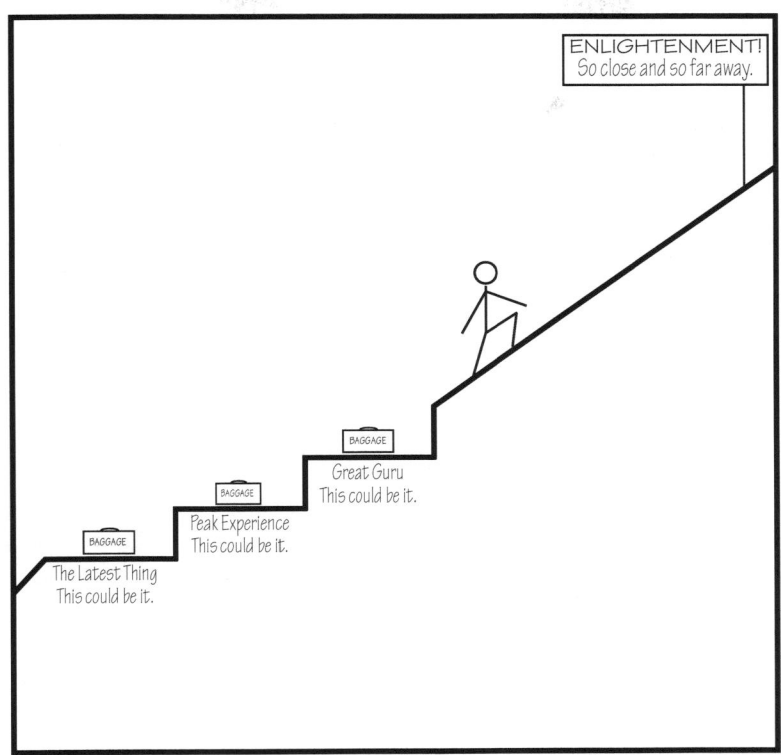

I try different paths.

Sometimes they bring me happiness
or peace
or contentment
for awhile.

Sometimes they reinforce my new identity as a
spiritual seeker.

Sometimes they help me let go
of some of my baggage.

Musings:

 Teachers and practices

There is another way in which practicing itself, almost regardless of what the particular practice is, can help one awaken.

A good teacher may use practices and exercises to help you move past your egoic or identity boundaries (your stories about who you are). When a teacher asks you to do something beyond your comfort level even when you do not feel like it, what they are saying is that this is a practice. I know that sounds obvious, but we are not a "practice" or "mastery" oriented culture. We (at least in the U.S.) do not much care for the idea of practicing. We claim to admire it in our athletes, while still being enamored of those who make something seem effortless—as if no practice was involved. We don't seem to have much respect for mastery either. We are too easily seduced by novelty. We want things to be new and instant and to come easy.

When we practice beyond our comfort zone it draws our attention to the illusion of our own identity. Our comfort zone is actually made up of the borders our ego has constructed. When ego (our identity) tells us that "we cannot do that." what it means is that "we cannot do that and maintain the illusion of who we are." The ego defends the illusion at all costs.

So even though the practice itself does not lead to awakening, if you are willing to toss your identity onto the bonfire in these moments of intense practice it shows you that you can actually cross those boundaries and not die.

The doer dies, but what is behind the doing lives.

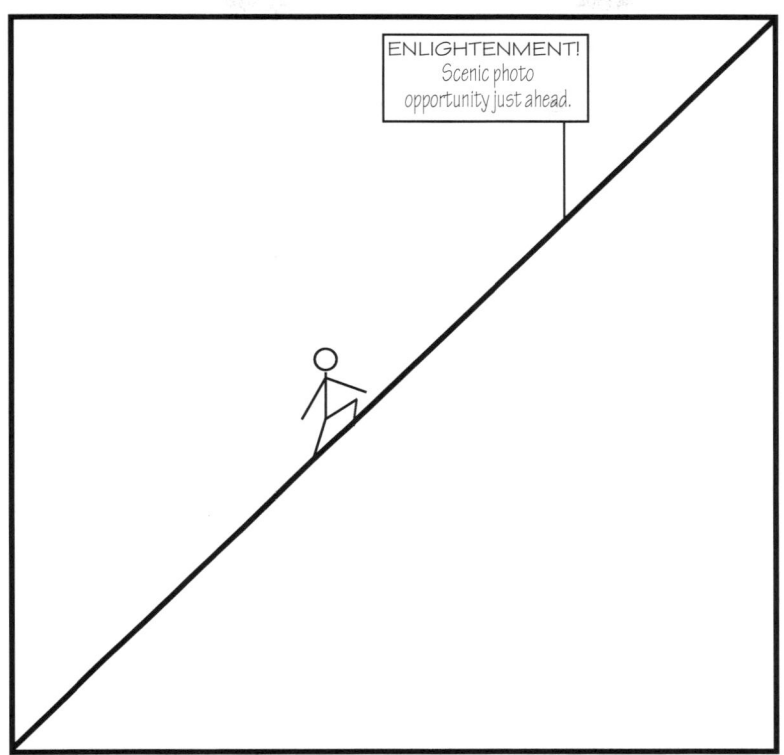

But it always comes back to
me and the mountain.

Sometimes I get angry.

After all,
I'm being spiritual,
I'm doing spiritual work,
I'm living spiritually,
so why is GOD making this so hard on me.

It's not fair!

Musings:

 Stories of enlightenment

GOD may be the ultimate science fantasy author. As the ultimate storyteller, GOD creates an illusion and to make this illusion believable, He/She creates rules and order, with which we try to understand our place and manipulate the outcome of the story in our favor. Even though the book is already written, it is not written for us until we turn the page and discover that whatever comes next is the only thing that could have come next in a perfect universe.

As long as we confine our attention to the story in which we find ourselves, one set of rules seem to apply—get stuff, find love, be happy. We believe that we are writing this story as we go and that there is an "I" that is acting in this drama.

When we start contemplating the nature of the storyteller, we call that being on a spiritual path. We can come to all kinds of spiritual accommodations with GOD the storyteller, but they all end up being illusory deals we make in order to influence the course of a story that is already written. "I'll be good. I'll be compassionate. I'll live by spiritual precepts if you'll promise to reward me in this life or the next."

The ultimate truth is that there is no separate us and no separate storytelling GOD and not even a story that has been written down. There is only a perfect dream without a dreamer, impressing words on a divine page as they arise in their absolute perfection.

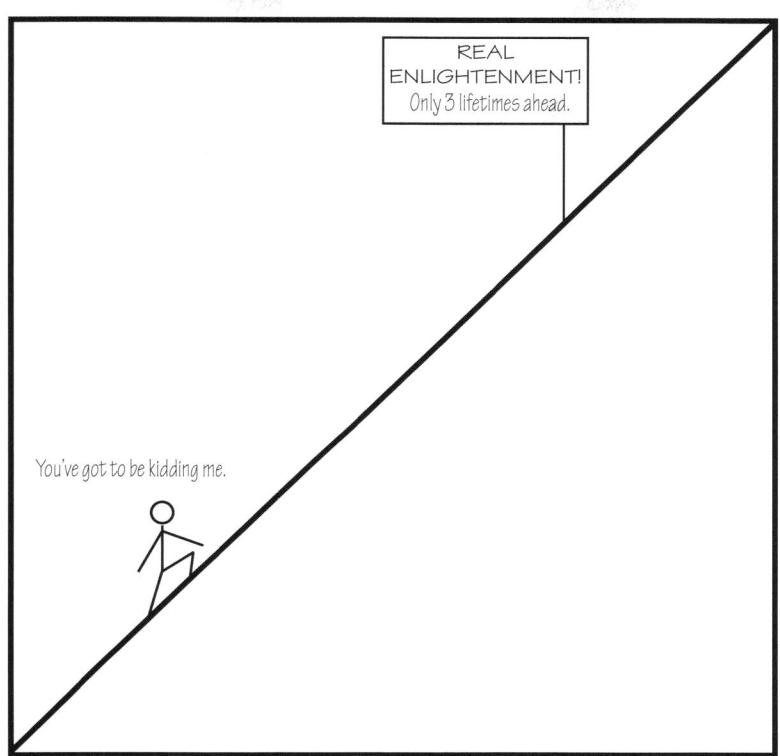

The mountain seems like it will go on forever.

I want to quit, but I've come so far.
I want to go back, but back to what?
I want to continue, but I question my capacity.

In this rarefied atmosphere
I begin to lose my sense of
who I am,
who I ever was.

And then...

Musings:

 The path of the expanding I

Most spiritual traditions that believe that the true nature of reality is nondual argue that it is a mistake to identify with anything or to form an ego identity at all. This is true but sometimes less than practical. To instantly go from a strong but limited sense of "I" to the dissolution of that sense is difficult and as likely to lead to a psychotic break or devolution into dysfunctionality as to enlightenment.

One might also argue that the natural evolution of our consciousness favors a kind of expansion of what we consider to be within our sphere of identity. We seem to be naturally self-centered and then evolve our capacity to love and care for the freedom of our family, and then friends and groups, and then a larger community and then ever larger spheres. In effect, we are expanding our identity.

By continually identifying with a greater and greater sense of "I," we can eventually come to identify with everything, which is much the same as identifying with nothing.

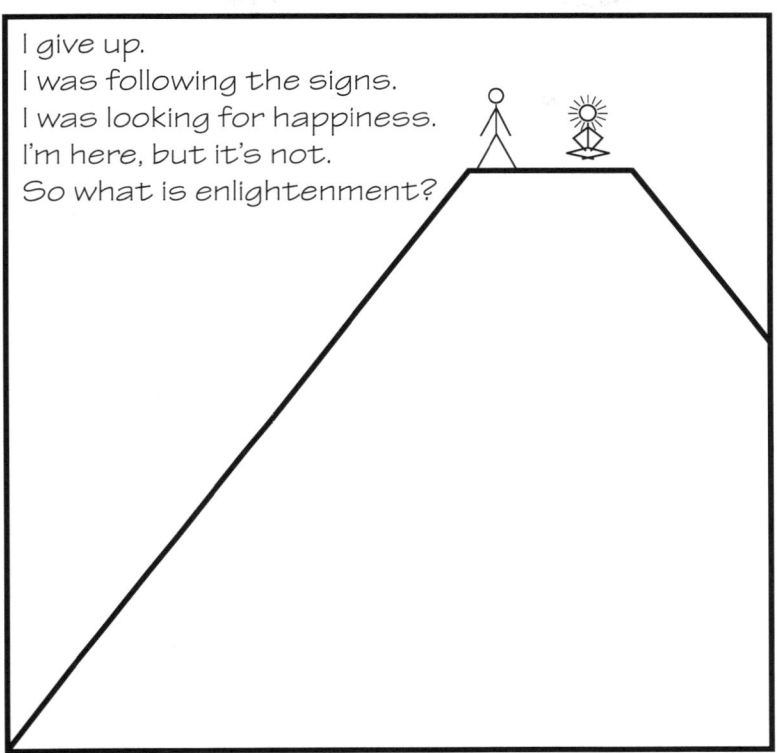

I give up.
I was following the signs.
I was looking for happiness.
I'm here, but it's not.
So what is enlightenment?

I'm there.

Or I'm here.

There is no place left to climb.

I'm at the top of the mountain
and it's just me and me.

I'm beyond confused.

Musings:

 Who am I?

Who am I?

Just ask the question.

Any answer you get will be a red herring, a false lead, the sign post and not the destination. The real purpose in asking the question is to feel into the space that opens up just after you ask the question and before the first answer arises.

Now ask the question again. Who am I?

A deeper answer will arise, but the deeper answer is just as much of an illusion. It arises to fill the uncomfortable void that our ego feels when we direct our attention to who we really are beyond all the stories. We can't stay in this space for very long, because it feels to our egos like death and total annihilation, so we ask the question again.

Who am I?

If the inquiry is deep enough and goes on long enough, we begin to run out of answers and the space that opens up between question and answer expands. Some say that one taste of that space can expand into an abiding.

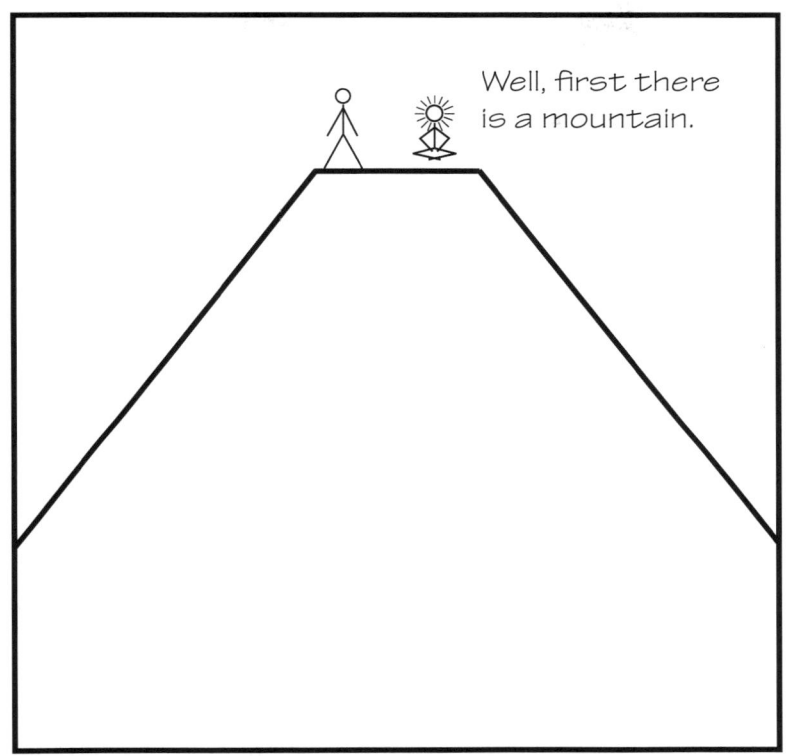

Well, first there
is a mountain.

Now I'm talking to myself.

And now I am answering.

This could be insanity.

Am I breaking down or breaking through?

Musings:

The Five Movements of pure awareness: Part 1

In the First Movement we are asleep and dreaming. Sometimes we have fleeting moments of awakening—a momentary experience of what is actually true or what the waking world is really like, but we mostly ignore those moments. Most people live most of their lives in the First Movement. Sometimes the dreams are good dreams and sometimes they are nightmares, but the First Movement is characterized by mistaking the illusion for the reality, the map for the territory, the transient identity for the deep source. We tend to view other people or situations as being the cause of our happiness or unhappiness and we are like puppets acting according to unconscious scripts. We intuit an incompleteness, but we seek completion in the material realm of things, experiences and circumstances.

The Second Movement is triggered by an intuition that the completion we are seeking will not be found in the manipulation of the external. We then spend a lot of energy either avoiding that intuition or redirecting our search.

The Second Movement is where we begin to pursue spiritual things. It is where spiritual seeking arises (though it can also be where material seeking reaches new heights as a kind of avoidance mechanism).

In the Second Movement we may experience tantalizing but fleeting peak experiences and moments of pure awareness. We develop a hunger for these experiences that both motivate us to spiritual practice and keep us convinced that pure awareness is a destination. We begin to understand that we play a critical role in shaping our own reality and defining our own states of suffering.

continued

But the quality of this conversation with myself
is very different.

This is not the constant mind chatter
of habitual patterns and filters
running over and over again
in my head.

This is me, turning my attention inward,
searching for the "I"
that has always seemed to be there,
and finding nothing.

Musings:

 The Five Movements of pure awareness:
Part 2

We may spend years in this Second Movement—tasting pure awareness and then losing it. We may have awakened moments in some areas or domains of our lives, but not in others. We may have mind-blowing, consciousness-altering, peak experiences and we may feel ourselves dissolving into a gooey puddle of warm fuzzy oneness, but that is not enlightenment. In fact, those peak experiences can end up being a trap. The challenge of the Second Movement is that we believe that there is something to be acquired or attained that will make us happy. We can get stuck as we engage in practices that refine our spiritual identities without piercing the veil of illusion that keeps us in suffering.

The Third Movement comes when we actually wake up to the true nature of reality and can abide there. This Third Movement is what is often classically called enlightenment. This is described by those who have attained it as either a profound peacefulness or a terrifying death to everything that we have spent a lifetime valuing. The "I" dissolves into the void that is pure consciousness and this dissolution can be blissful or horrible.

Real enlightenment is a strange state because it is so radically contrary to the human condition. Without preferences we don't value eating over not eating. We don't value survival and safety over death or danger. We don't need anything anymore. If we live we live, if we die, we die. We care about this about as much as we would care about ice melting into water or water evaporating into steam. It is simply a state change for our consciousness, which is, of course, the only real thing.

continued

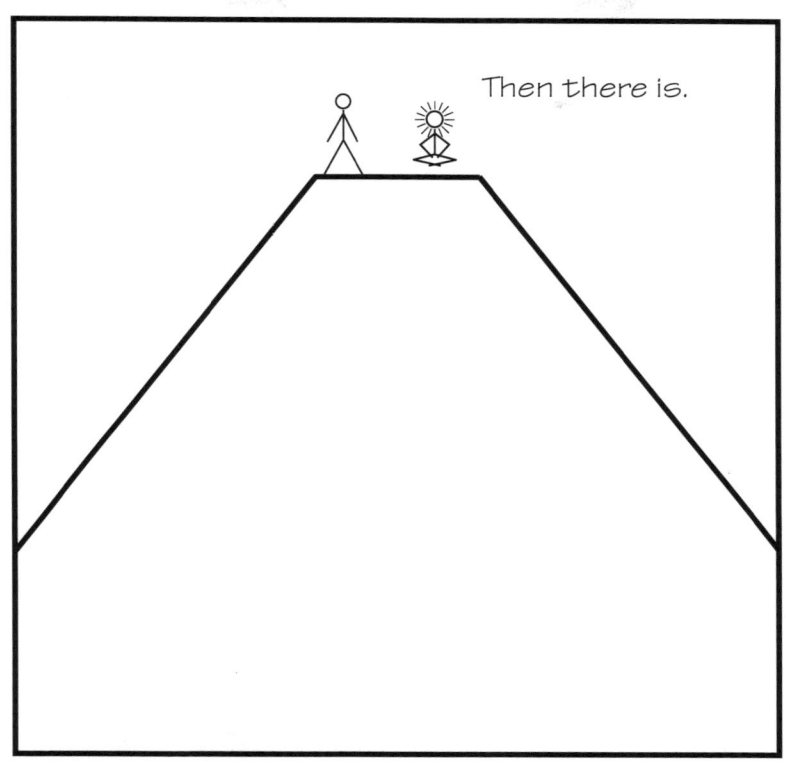

Then there is.

This is inquiry.

This is facing what I find
as honestly as I can.

When I turn inward to find the "I"
that has always seemed to be there,
what I find is the mystery.

And the only honest way to face the mystery
is with awe and wonder and curiosity.

That is inquiry.

Musings:

 The Five Movements of pure awareness:
Part 3

Actual awakening is a strange and intense experience. It is not surprising that so many people can't sustain it from a state of consciousness into a stage. It is not an intellectual position. It can be extremely hard on those who orbit around us. In the Third Movement we love everyone with the same intensity, which can make it feel like we love no one, because we are not demonstrating preferences anymore. We love every child as much as our own child. We love every man or woman as much as we love our intimate partner. Our love is not exclusive and directional. It beams out in all directions.

This stage is not really conducive to the survival of the physical form, but then that physical form is seen to be an impermanent illusion anyway. The Third Movement is the emergence of the nondual self and the disappearance of the dual self. Dwelling in this space usually requires a support network or a community because it is hard to live this way and interact with the world. It may be that the idea of withdrawing from the world came as a natural reaction to the Third Movement.

But as radical and as important as this Third Movement is, it is not the end game. As the Zen saying goes, "first there is a mountain, then there is no mountain, then there is." In the First and Second Movements of pure awareness, there is a mountain. More precisely, there appears to be a mountain. It is a mountain that needs to be climbed or a mountain that is a barrier or a mountain that defines your story and your choices. In the Third Movement, almost all at once, there is no mountain. For some, this enlightened state is the supreme state, but there is a Fourth Movement and that is when, all at once, there is a mountain again.

continued

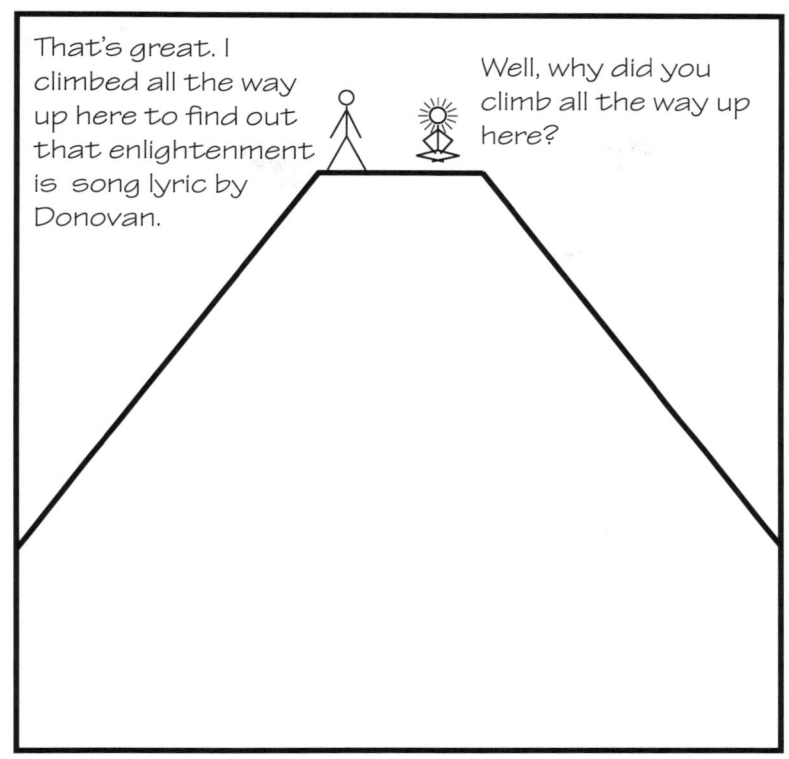

Of course,
just because I'm now asking myself
the right questions
does not mean that I'm enlightened.

In fact,
I could end up as confused as I ever was.
Especially since I keep hoping
for a straight answer
but all I get are statements
pointing me back to me.

Musings:

 The Five Movements of pure awareness: Part 4

If we are not so lucky as to have the support system to dwell in wakeful nirvana or if we simply choose the Bodhisattva's path of working for the enlightenment of all beings, then the mountain will reappear. Earthly concerns, preferences, attachments, stories, and identities will all return. The yearning for relationship, the desire for love, the preference for beauty, the urge to create, and the drive to add love or consciousness to the world will return, but there will be no self to experience them.

Any pain we felt in the First and Second Movements will be amplified in the Fourth Movement because we will not be feeling our "personal" pain, we will be feeling the pain of the whole world and it will be excruciating. We will allow this pain to move through us and we will not add suffering to the mix. Where pain in the First and Second Movements required fault and meaning because we were a victim of it—it was happening to us—pain in the Fourth Movement elicits compassion. In the Fourth Movement, we experience the return of the illusory world, but now it is like a reflection without a mirror.

The Fourth Movement is what happens when you move from the radically non-attached state of "no mountains" back to the world in which wood still needs to be chopped and water still needs to be carried. The Fifth Movement corresponds to a complete integration of the dual and the nondual self. If, for instance, you let love animate the shell that was once "you" in order to paint the world with love or if you allow consciousness to pour from the vessel with which you once identified in order to take the world deep into awakened consciousness and absolute freedom, then you are living the Fifth Movement.

continued

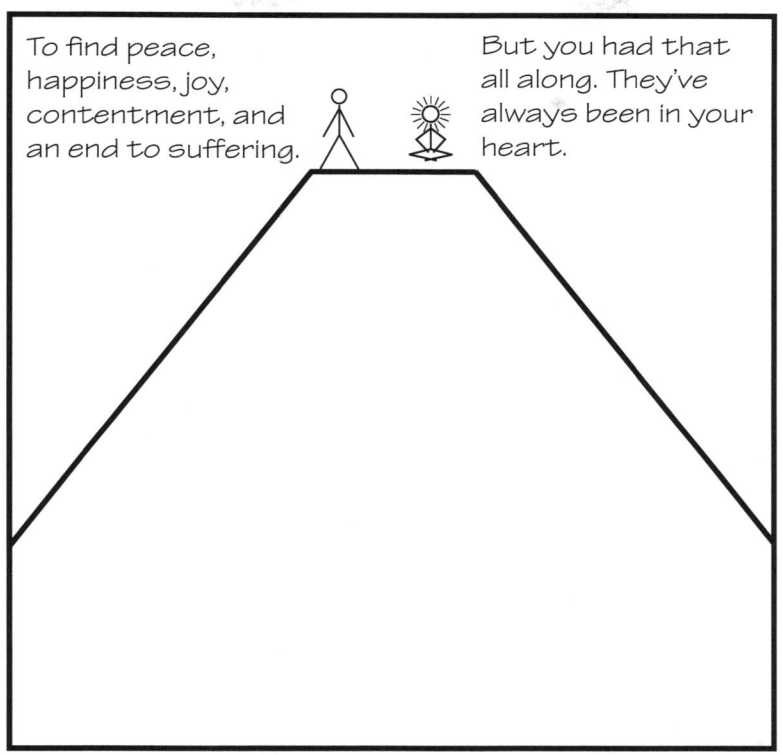

To find peace, happiness, joy, contentment, and an end to suffering.

But you had that all along. They've always been in your heart.

See what I mean.

It's like I'm Dorothy in the Wizard of Oz.
I could have had my heart's desire all along.
I could have gone home at any time.
I could have woken up at any time.

Great!

But I still don't know how!

Would someone please
just give me the ruby slippers.

Musings:

 The Five Movements of pure awareness: Part 5

The Fifth Movement is the integration of pure awareness and active compassion. Where the Third Movement was about giving up the game, the Fifth Movement is about playing the game with full consciousness, pure awareness, and absolute compassion. The Fifth Movement is when you have awakened to the fact that the true nature of the world is oneness, that all separate forms are illusory AND you decide to allow consciousness to play through you as an art form and serve through you as an expression of the perfection that is.

In the Fifth Movement we recognize that the desire and preferences and attachments we feel do not define us. They are not who we are and they do not lead anywhere. We choose to feel because that is the great gift of this incarnation. We do not distract ourselves from what we are feeling. We live a fully engaged life from an awakened perspective. We may choose to become attached to things in the wakeful and conscious awareness that we will experience pain when those attachments dissolve. Both the Third and the Fifth Movements might be characterized by a lack of suffering, but where the Third Movement eliminates suffering by eliminating attachment, the Fifth Movement eliminates suffering by engaging the world with consciousness and compassion.

Of course, all of this is just a story. It's just words pointing in the direction of something that is beyond words. Don't hold too tightly to any idea of how things must be.

In one sense, there is an enlightenment that I will never know because to achieve it would mean the end of the separate me that could perceive that I had attained it. From that vantage point, it appears that enlightenment does not actually exist.

In another sense there is an enlightenment that has always been within me, a kind of capacity to recognize my true nature and the true nature of reality itself. It was never something I needed to find or acquire. I am not less of who I am when I'm dreaming and I do not need to find or improve myself in order to wake up.

Musings:

 Time

Actually, there's only one instant, and it's right now.

And it's eternity.

And it's an instant in which God is posing a question.

And that question is, basically, "Do you want to, you know, be one with eternity? Do you want to be in heaven?"

And we're all saying, "No, thank you. Not just yet."

And so time is actually just this constant saying no to God's invitation.

From the film *Waking Life* by Richard Linklater (2001)

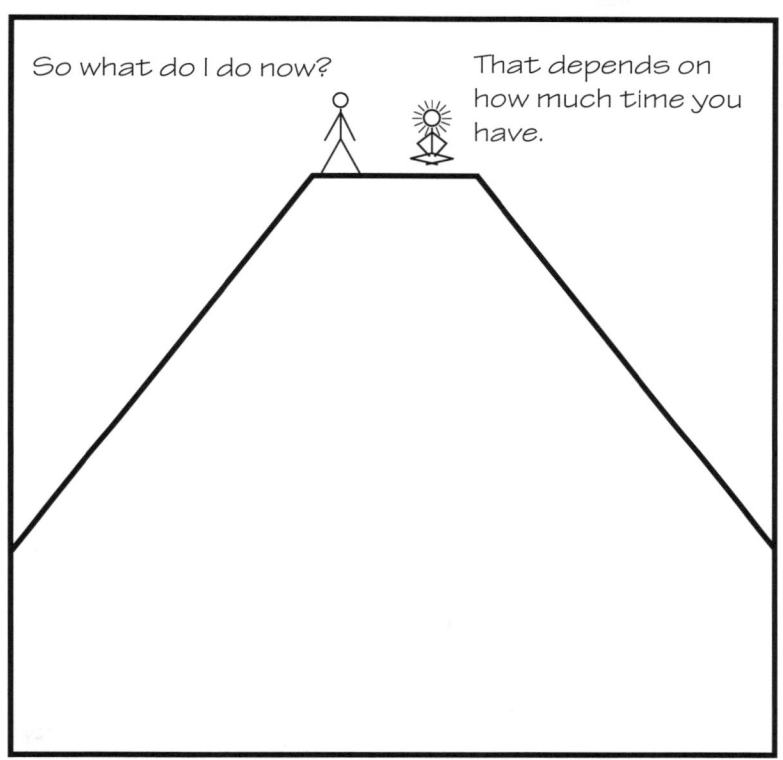

Well, the honest answer is that I don't know
how much time I have.

I mean maybe I believe I have multiple lifetimes
to figure this out,
but I don't know that for certain.

I got here, wherever here is,
because "happy enough" was not enough.
I was driven to this point
because I was exhausted by being driven.

Yes, I know how strange that sounds.

Musings:

 Waking up

We don't wake up easily. We hit that snooze button as many times as we possibly can until we can't pretend to be asleep any longer.

Maybe money will make me happy—snooze button.
Maybe success will make me happy—snooze button.
Maybe power will make me happy—snooze button.
Maybe the perfect lover will make me happy—snooze button.
Maybe God will make me happy—snooze button.
Maybe, maybe, maybe,
snooze button, snooze button, snooze button,
fuck, fuck, fuck.

Who set this fucking alarm anyway? Well, I'm awake now! Awake and pissed off!

There is no "happy" outside of me. Happiness is a destination at which I will never arrive. So now what? Sit around and be unhappy? Well, if there is no "happy" outside of me, then there can be no "unhappy" outside of me. So if I'm sitting around being unhappy in myself, I might just as easily kill this time until I die by sitting around being "happy" in myself.

And, if by some miracle, I actually start living that—simply being happy, until I'm not and then letting whatever other feelings that arise wash through me without clinging to them, until I return to happy again—then maybe I'm not as empty and needful as I thought I was. Maybe I can just offer myself up in service as a creative way of killing time until I die and dissolve back into the oneness from which I arose.

Mind you, I'm no longer serving to find anything or get anything. I'm just serving because I've woken up in this garden whose flowers seem to need water and I am water.

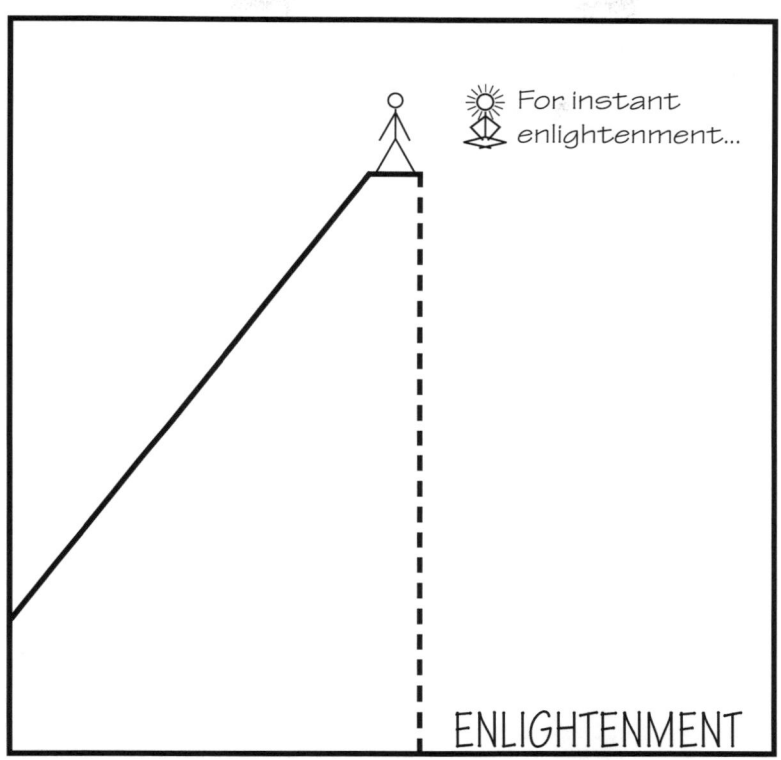

I used to think that I was afraid of heights,
but I've realized that it is not the height
that I am afraid of.

I am afraid of the edge.

I am afraid that some force beyond my control:
a gust of wind;
the hand of GOD;
my own karma;
my own curiosity;
will push me over the edge
before I'm ready.

Musings:

 The death of the seeker

The death of the seeker is the falling away of separation. What falls away is the sense of lack. This life is already enough. This has always been here, and this is all there is.

The word nirvana has a literal meaning of "the blowing out of a candle or flame," but this implies a doing—a choice to extinguish the flame of identity. But the original etymology of nirvana probably originated in the idea that the fire in the forge of a blacksmith would go out if the bellows stopped blowing air across it—feeding the flame. This gives us a different meaning. It is in the cessation of the act of blowing (constantly directing attention to and identifying with) that the flame of identity dies away.

Beyond that it gets confusing to talk about the differentiated meanings for the word nirvana that have come down to us through various Hindu and Buddhist sects and schools. The discussion can be fascinating, but it often feels like it is talking "around" what is essential, like Biblical scholars arguing over how many angels can dance on the head of a pin.

What does seem useful is the underlying sense that our ideas about who we are, whether they are psychological ideas or spiritual ideas, all depend upon the concept of a separate and independent self. If that sense of "I" disappears, then so too the foundation for a psychological or a spiritual conception of the self.

The death of the seeker is also the death of religion and spirituality and GOD. It is a return to the simple arising of what is.

There are risks either way.

I can leap and awaken now
perhaps plunging into madness or even death.

I can practice and perhaps gradually awaken
or delude myself with lifetimes of saying
"No, I'm not quite ready,"
to GOD's invitation.

And, of course, both choices are illusions.

Musings:

 The boat across the river

Buddhism can be seen as a spiritual path of letting go. Buddhists let go of attachment, or at least they are supposed to. They let go of the illusions that keep them in suffering. Ultimately, however, they must also let go of Buddhism itself.

The Buddha said that the awakened state is like the opposite bank of a river. Buddhism, the dharma, is like the boat you take to cross that river. But once you have crossed that river, you don't need the boat anymore. You can let go of the boat. You can let go of Buddhism itself.

I've come where few people travel
in order to find what I had with me all along.

And ultimately the question is
how will I live this life
once I fully embody the truth
that there is no separate me?

What will happen to the dream
once I know that I am dreaming it?

What life am I going back to?

Musings:

 The mountain and the path:
Part 1

So what do you do when you get to the top of the very tall mountain only to find that paradise (enlightenment) is in the valley far below? You will find yourself with what are essentially two paths. The first leads over the sheer cliff and is the fastest and most instant path to the oneness of paradise and enlightenment. It is also the most terrifying because it means we give up control and dive in and everything changes, everything dies.

Some people find themselves at that precipice after such a breakdown and such a long dark night of the soul and in such pain that they simply leap and it is either enlightenment or madness. These are where the stories of instant enlightenment often come from (though instant is never really instant when you consider the amount of time spent in suffering and confusion it took to get to the precipice).

The second path is the long and winding road down the mountain. This path is slower and safer, but is fraught with its own challenges. Because it is slow, we sometimes feel we are not making progress and so we deviate from the path and try shortcuts or find that we have just been wasting time with a detour that has actually not taken us any closer to the valley.

Some people find this path so long and so tiring that they just set up camp somewhere along the trail and decide to call that spot "the valley" (as if they have already made it). If enough other travelers decide to join them, they can create a little mountain town in which they all agree that this is the valley and they have all reached enlightenment. This is of course, a delusion, but for some of us, we need to spend time in delusion to rest, before moving on with our journey.

continued

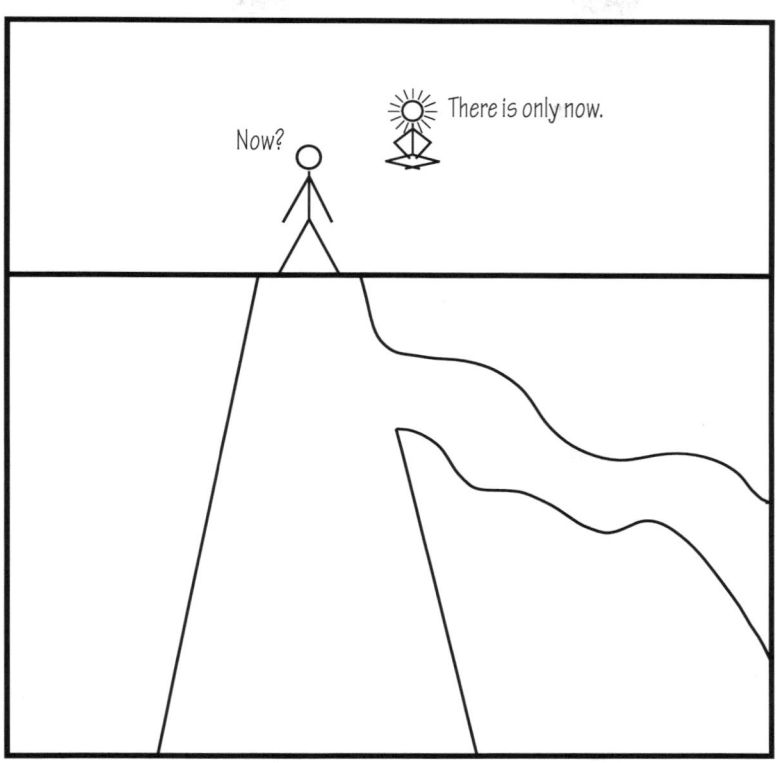

I've spent a lifetime trying to win a game
whose rules I do not
and probably could not ever
fully understand.

I've spent a lifetime preparing for a contest
that I'm pretty sure I'm going to fail.

The realization that the game and the contest
are all just part of a dream
I've been dreaming,
is not as comforting as I thought it would be.

Musings:

 The mountain and the path:
Part 2

While some people may cling to this little delusion or that little delusion, others eventually wake up to the illusory quality of the little wayside town and begin their journey again.

Of course the long mountain path also brings us continually back to the sheer cliff face that overlooks the valley below. We always have the option to leap or to simply awaken, but precious few of us are brave enough or desperate enough for that choice. We say that we want the melting embrace of oneness, we want to "let go and let God," we want to dissolve past all our carefully constructed boundaries, but just not quite yet.

The sheer cliff is a metaphor for abandoning all our strategies. It is terrifying. As terrifying as it would be in real life if someone took you to that real cliff face and said "Trust me. Jump and you will wake up from the illusion."

What kind of promises would you need—what assurances— before making the leap? Honestly, I don't think many of us would make that leap. I think that some of us who think we made that leap or think we are making that leap, may well wake up in one of those mountain villages of delusion rather than in the valley of enlightenment.

It's hard for me to judge people for that. If it was easy, we would all be doing it.

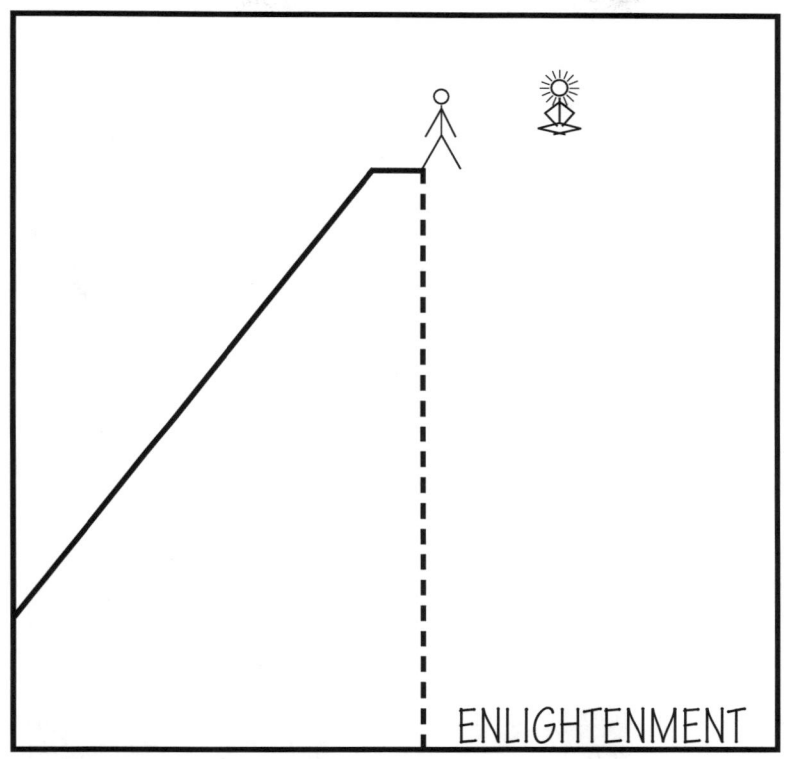

ENLIGHTENMENT

But if this is a dream
and this is my chance to wake up...

If all there is
is now
and the appearance of a choice
between now or later
is just an illusion...

If the game can't continue without my saying,
"Yes..."

Musings:

 The Cycle of birth and death

The book we know in the West as **"The Tibetan Book of The Dead,"** *is actually titled* **"The Great Liberation upon Hearing in the Intermediate State"** *or, more succinctly,* **"The Great Book of Natural Liberation."** *The Tibetans believe that at the moment of death, you are far wiser than you were in life. In this "intermediate state" you are more open to hearing and realizing the truth of your nondual nature. So by having this text read aloud to you after death, you might achieve the great liberation. In death is the great release and relaxation into the true nondual nature of reality.*

The second reason for having this ancient text read aloud to the now empty vessel of consciousness (the corpse) is that we spend so little time in life actually awake to the reality of our true nature, that when we die, our consciousness often clings to old forms and old concepts and we tend to wander the bardos (realms of consciousness) lost and confused (or worse—frightened and disoriented).

The Tibetans say that when we are born into this realm we cry, but the world is joyful at our arrival. And when we die, the world cries over our departure, but we may find our greatest joy.

The thing about falling
is that pretty much everything else disappears.

My past is not flashing before my eyes.
I am not fantasizing about the future.

I remember that I loved someone once.
I remember that I was loved.

That's all there is time for.

Musings:

 A taste of enlightenment:
Part 1

This may sound like a radical pronouncement, but I'm going to suggest that the thing we call enlightenment or awakening or realization is always a state change in our consciousness rather than a permanent stage change. In other words, by its very nature it is temporary. First of all to become enlightened suggests a moment of being in darkness—that the moment before I became enlightened, I was in darkness.

Enlightenment, awakening, and realization all suggest a moment of transition out of darkness, sleep or an unrealized state into something new. But from within that new state (however long it lasts) the old state and the new state are not seen as separate states but as one. So using terms like enlightenment or awakening or realization is actually merely a convention that we use to describe something we anticipate or desire (or dread).

Imagine that the state you most desired was to be unencumbered and unburdened from gravity, to awaken, as it were, to the truth that gravity is an illusion. If I were to jump on a trampoline, I might have the peak experience of being free from gravity in the moment where my ascension had reached its zenith and my descent had not yet begun. In that moment, we are, in fact, fully weightless and free. We cannot be any more weightless in that fraction of a second. This taste of being free of gravity is similar to the peak experiences of enlightenment (the truth of nonduality) that many of us have experienced though meditation, prayer, sexual union, or under the influence of plant spirit medicines, chemicals, or energetically charismatic individuals. In those moments of enlightenment we are fully enlightened and we cannot be more enlightened.

continued

Something strange happens
when there is only time for love.

You sometimes see it in people near to death,
people who have literally run out of time.

And I don't mean
the romantic possessive form of love.

I mean that recognition that GOD,
the beloved, the stuff that I am made from,
is in everyone I meet—
everyone I could ever meet.

Musings:

 A taste of enlightenment:
Part 2

The challenge is that, like the trampoline, the effects of our peak experiences of enlightenment are temporary. They comes to an end. Then we are left with a nagging to desire to have the experience again. Sometimes we become obsessed with a particular path like the trampoline. We keep bouncing and bouncing for years in the hopes that it will become permanent. We speak very authoritatively of our experiences, but they don't seem to transfer beyond the moment of bouncing.

Some of us hope that by extending the time we spend in weightlessness, we will become truly liberated from gravity. Perhaps we try diving underwater. This, like a meditation retreat for enlightenment, makes the experience seem to last longer, but we cannot escape the artificiality of the situation. We know that without an elaborate support network, we would simply drown.

The truth about gravity is that it is a perception attached to the body in which you incarnated. Truly escaping from the bounds of gravity is as simple as allowing the body that perceives gravity to die. If I was blindfolded and jumped from a plane, the transition from being in a body that was not perceiving the effects of gravity (because of the temporary freefall experience) to no longer having a body that perceived the effects of gravity would probably be pretty seamless, but that isn't what most people who pursue weightless states seem to want.

It is much the same for what we call enlightenment or awakening. Truly awakening in a way that affects us for more than just peak moments means the death of the one that perceives duality and there are two problems with that. First of all, most people are not ready for that kind ego or identity death, any

continued

So I first had to experience the mountain
I was dreaming as a real thing.

I had to climb that mountain and seek happiness
outside of myself until I had exhausted
all of my options.

I had to build a sense of myself that was so solid
and so separate that I could be certain that
more solidness and more separation
would not bring me happiness.

Then I had to awaken to the fact
that there was no mountain.

Musings:

 A taste of enlightenment:
Part 3

more than they are ready for their physical death. Second, in a realm in which the common language is duality, the perception of duality (as a conscious choice) can still be very useful. Gravity may ultimately be an illusion, but it can be a practical advantage to know what is likely to happen in this realm if I step off a high cliff.

Enlightenment, awakening and realization are words we use to describe a threshold experience. Sometimes we come to the threshold, survey the territory on the other side and turn back. Most of the time our relationship to enlightenment is then that we know about it, we feel it, or we have an intuition of it. But what does it mean to cross that threshold? I think the popular conception is that everything changes and we live in a blissful state of bemused detachment. But what if nothing changes other than what once seemed solid and separate and certain, now seems ephemeral and illusive and temporary? What if, on the other side of that threshold experience we call enlightenment, the "knowing about" that we once experienced gets transformed into a pure gnosis—a "knowing of?"

We might still live a life in a realm of duality, but we would live it with the deep compassion that comes from recognition.

But now that I know the mountain
to be a dream that I was dreaming,
or
now that I know the mountain and myself
to be made of the same dream-stuff,
I can see the mountain again.

I can live lucidly.

Not two.

Non dual.

Musings:

 The Illusion

I take my son to see a magic show.

We watch as the magician places the beautiful assistant in the long box. We see her head protruding from one end of the tight narrow box and her feet protruding from the other end.

The magician takes a great saw and with dramatic flair begins to cut the box in half. Playing her role well, the assistant looks anxious.

I feel wonder at the completeness of the illusion and curiosity about how it is done. I have no fear. Any tension I feel is a kind of joyful expectation. I laugh.

My child feels suspense and fear. He knows enough to know that being cut in half will cause pain. He begins to cry and protest. He wants it all to stop.

We are watching the same event, but it is eliciting very different responses. I understand the illusion. He does not.

But then the trick is completed and the woman who was sawed in half is restored to wholeness. He understands that it is a trick and that nothing bad has happened to the beautiful assistant. Now he wants to see it again and again and his fear is transformed into joyous curiosity and wonder.

He has had his first awakening.

Ahhh!

First there is a mountain, then there is no mountain, then there is.

There is no I, but there is wakefulness.
There is an I-shaped balloon, blown up with love.

Sometimes I slip on the "me" costume
just to play the role I was born to play.

But I am actor and audience and theater
all rolled into one,
saying lines that arise from the core consciousness
that is producer and playwright.

I am the dream and the dreamer.

Chapter Five

He Said, She Said
Nonduality for Couples

When I look deeply inward
I discover that I am nothing
but consciousness.

When I look deeply outward
I realize that I am nothing
but love.

Musings:

 Nonduality for two

Nowhere does the conflict between desire and desire-less-ness or form and formlessness seem more palpable than in the realm of intimate relationships between couples.

In fact most of the images we have of enlightened or awakened beings are of individuals who have renounced community and relationship to live isolated lives as hermits or in a monastic existence where the complications of intimate relationship do not intrude. Many, if not most, of the religious or spiritual traditions of the East and the West suggest that a choice needs to be made between GOD and an intimate companion in this incarnation. People who speak about nonduality often seem curiously asexual, as if transcending the separate self means denying the face of the beloved.

This bias might reflect the fact that those who have traditionally had the most to say about nonduality are those who have come from celibate or monastic traditions. They may actually have little experience and not much to say about nonduality in relationship, but I don't believe that means that a relationship based in the truth of nondual awareness is impossible. It is difficult, but not impossible.

When we recognize the lack of separation between ourselves and another, we call that love. This is neither romantic love, nor erotic love, nor platonic love, though it may encompass them all. Love as a recognition of the unity of all form is deeper than that. It holds the possibility of transcendence and even awakening, but it may be the trickiest and most confusing of all the paths to pure awareness.

Remember this line?

Yes, this is still GOD.
This line is still everything.
This line is the all-embracing wholeness of reality.

The line is complete in itself.

Musings:

 Which comes first?

Ultimately, nonduality is a simple concept. It is in fact so simple that it is radically difficult for us to even conceive of. In order to conceive of it, we tend to use stories that make it seem like we can separate from the process or that there was something from which we could separate.

One of the deepest stories we carry in our genetic memory is that it appears to us as though two separate beings must come together and mix their essences (masculine and feminine) in an affirmation or recognition of the underlying state of oneness in order to create new life (another separate form).

Notice in the illustration to the right that I have not drawn an upward facing triangle (masculine form) first and then added a downward facing triangle (feminine form), or vice versa. I have drawn them together, arising at the same moment out of the infinite ground of line (GOD). In many religions there is a story about whether the masculine or the feminine manifestation comes first. From a nondual awareness, however, this is not really a question.

In order for a masculine or a feminine something to arise, each needs to arise out of nothingness. Each needs to arise simultaneously with its polar opposite. Otherwise, there would be no knowing it—no recognizing it as something unique.

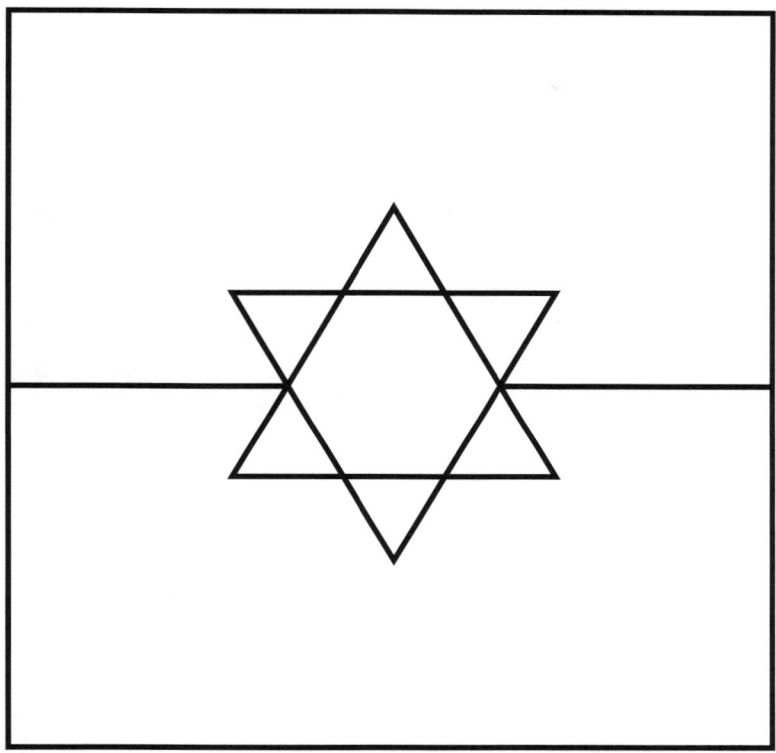

And...

Another way of thinking about this line
is as a divine pair.

The masculine △ and the feminine ▽,
embracing and entangling
in undifferentiated bliss.

Musings:

 To know the other

In the Bible the phrase "he knew her" or "she knew him or "they knew each other" is commonly interpreted to mean sexual intimacy, but there is a deeper meaning. To know someone is to have a knowing (a gnosis) of that person. But this "knowing" is not a surface knowing of "I know about you," or "I know how you appear," or "I know the details that make you seem to be similar to or distinct from me," or "I know the degree to which you align with my sexual preferences." This knowing is ultimately about a recognition that we are one. We can, of course, engage in sexual intercourse or intimacy without experiencing this recognition, but we cannot know the other as the self without it.

The deeper the recognition is, the more profound the nature of the sexual experience will be and the more profound the nature of the sexual experience, the deeper the sense of dissolution of separateness is likely to be.

One or both partners sometimes experience this sense of dissolution during sex and it can be very powerful. Unfortunately we are only capable of understanding an altered state of consciousness like this from the stage of consciousness we are currently at. Sometimes that means that we come to believe that the feeling, the awareness of no separation, was a result of the sex rather than a feeling we have access to at any moment and then transcendent sex becomes just another thing that we add to our list of things or experiences we are seeking.

You might be more familiar with the image of the
divine masculine and feminine expressed in this
form from Tibetan Buddhist Tangkas.

The Shiva/Buddha form (masculine)
has his eyes open as pure consciousness
and true identity.

The Shakti/Buddha form (feminine)
has her eyes closed or half closed in total bliss
because she has not yet become aware
of a state of separateness.

Musings:

 Polarity and nonduality

The reason that sexuality and intimate love is such a challenge to the idea of nonduality, and probably the reason why most spiritual traditions (with the notable exception of tantra) have simply taken it off the table, is that sexual attraction is fueled by the appearance of polarity, which means the play of amplifying differences, or, in nondual terms, illusions.

Despite whether it is politically correct to admit this, there are qualities that form polarities (meaning we cannot be exhibiting both qualities simultaneously). At one end of the scale are qualities that have traditionally been described as feminine and at the other end are qualities that have been described as masculine. The more a person animates and expresses those masculine qualities, the more it will attract a person animating or expressing more feminine qualities and vice versa. This balancing act is the source of sexual attraction.

It sounds logical that we would be most compatible with someone who is very much like us and that may well be true in the long run, but simple compatibility does not create the bonding that strong initial attraction does. Like it or not, we will be more powerfully attracted to those who polarize us. A person who is very purposeful and directed will attract and be attracted to someone who is open to being directed. A person who is expressing a full spectrum of energy will attract and be attracted to someone capable of great depth of feeling and penetration.

Shakti attracts Shiva precisely because she is his polar opposite. She offers her energy and vibration and movement (her dance) to his consciousness and spaciousness and stillness (his presence) and together they remember their fundamental unity.

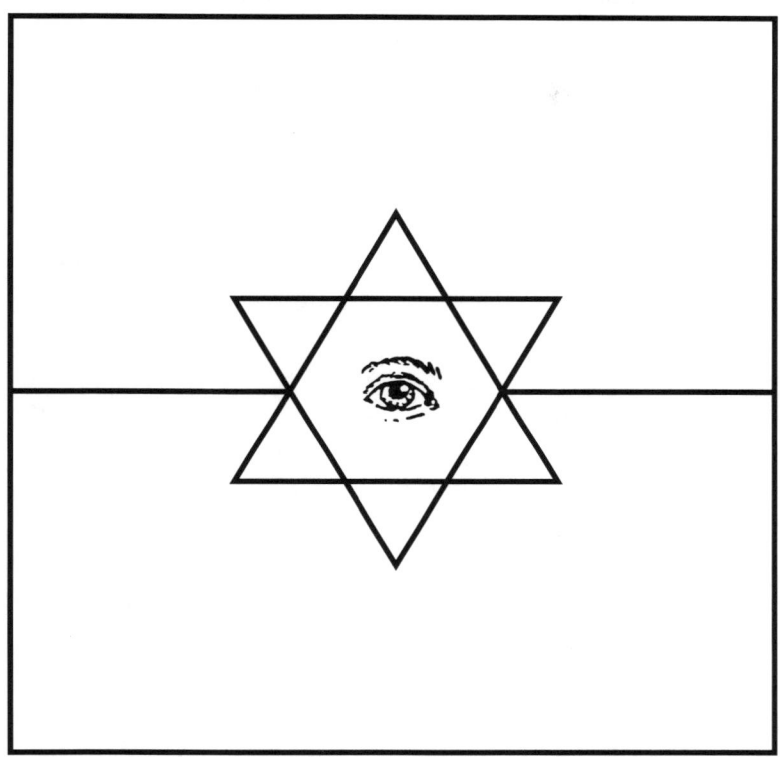

At this point there is still no separation.

Well, technically, there is already
all kinds of separation
going on here.

To even conceive of this
we need to imagine a phenomenon
and an observer of that phenomenon.

But let's not make this more complicated
than it needs to be right now.

Musings:

 The polarity game

While polarity is often expressed in masculine and feminine terms, it is not synonymous with the gender distinction of male and female. Any man or woman at any moment is either: habitually (because of an egoic defense mechanism), or developmentally (because of a natural expansion of capacity) or consciously (as a practice and an art form) identifying with a more masculine, or more feminine set of qualities in the spectrum of masculine and feminine expression, though masculine or feminine is still, fundamentally, not what you are.

Any male or female is completely capable of expressing the full spectrum of masculine and feminine energy. Some women may even express masculine energy more profoundly then some men and some men may express feminine energy more profoundly than some women, and, any man or woman also has a natural resting place on this energetic spectrum where they tend to go when they are completely open and relaxed as love. Granted, this is still just an appearance, but it will appear that way before awakening and after awakening, though it may appear differently after awakening.

Learning to work with this natural force of attraction and energetic expression means coming to rest and relax in the place on that spectrum from which you are most fully able to give your deepest gifts, while at the same time developing the artistry to utilize the full spectrum of masculine and feminine expression to open the hearts of others as a gift of service.

This will not make you happier or more enlightened. It will make you a more sensitive and energetically artful lover and it may prepare the ground for more transcendent experiences of bliss, but bliss is not what enlightenment is all about.

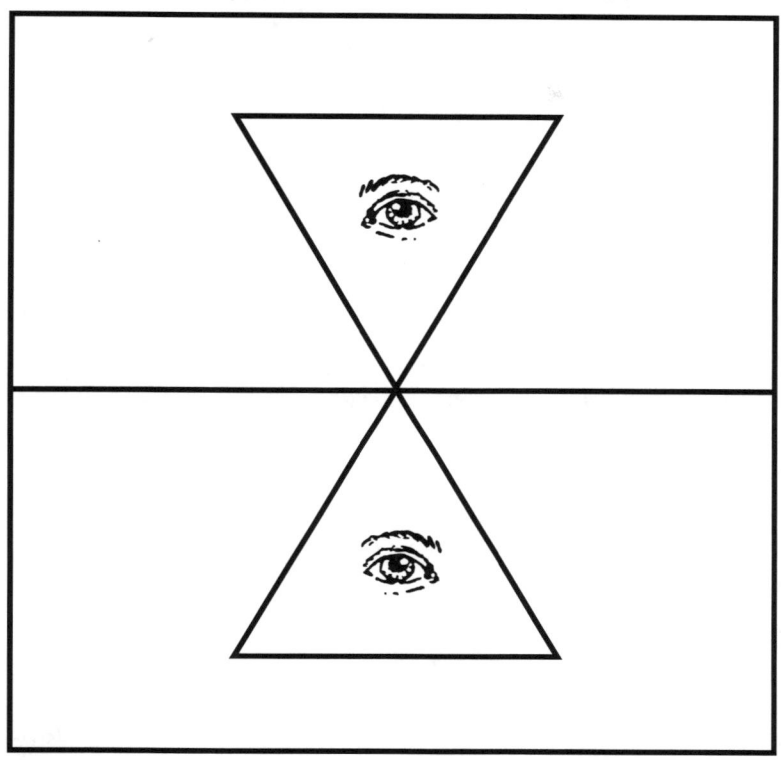

The next unfoldment into the realm of form
requires that the masculine and the feminine
become aware of their distinct nature.

They are still joined in union,
but they are aware of "other."

In one respect, the first illusion is a mirror.

Musings:

 Dream relationships

How often have you heard someone express the desire for or even wished that you yourself had a "dream relationship?" Well the problem is that "dream relationships" are exactly what we tend to attract.

From a nondual perspective, a "dream relationship" is any time a separate self wants to form a relationship with another separate self. Of course dream relationships are motivated by a desire to actually lose the separate sense of self and relax the constriction of incompleteness, but by their very nature, they are problematic.

1. *Any time we speak of being made whole, being completed, or finding our one and only soul mate, we are basing our relationship on a delusion. Placing the responsibility for our wholeness and our ability to love into the hands of another is unfair to that person and to ourselves. We are already complete in ourselves. That form we perceive as the perfect "other" may give us a sense of completeness for a time, but it will not last, unless we find our own sense of completeness that does not depend upon another.*

2. *The moment our happiness depends on the behavior or actions or existence of another, or on the permanence of that relationship, is the moment that we are throwing away the keys to our own prison door. It puts a shelf life on our happiness.*

3. *Our ideas about what we need a soul mate to be usually only reinforce our egoic constriction around a limited sense of a separate self. Our stories about ourselves require partners whose appearance and stories support our own stories.*

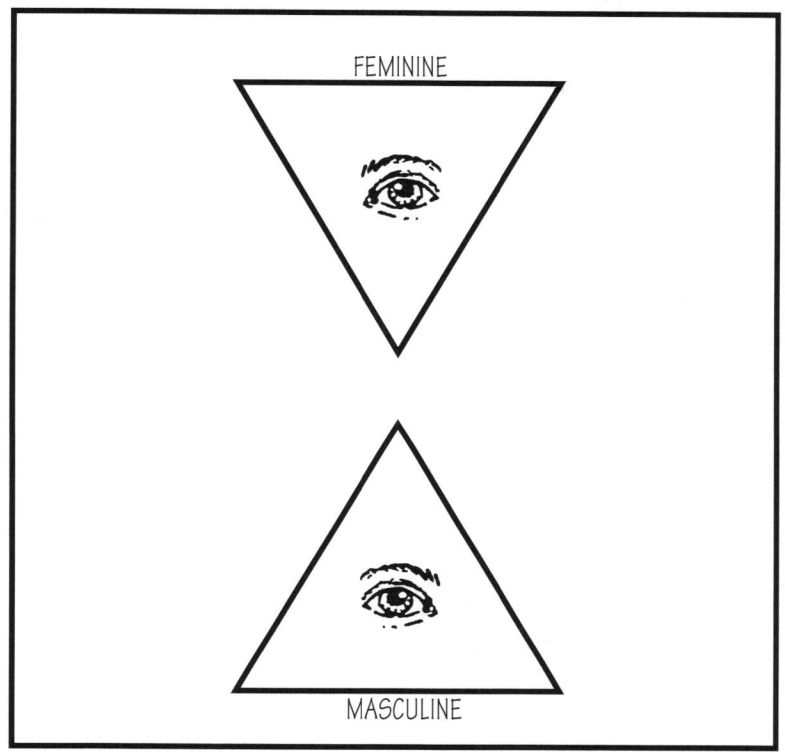

In separation,
the feminine assumes the role of object
or phenomenon
or thing that can be observed.

The masculine assumes the role of subject
or the ground upon which phenomenon unfolds
or the observer.

Musings:

 Lucid dream relationships

A "dream relationship" is characterized by both partners seeking to have their own egoic needs met (identities reinforced) by the other. The stories we have about ourselves have both conscious and subconscious components.

We may consciously identify with a self that must be loved, seen, cherished, respected, obeyed, felt, supported, followed, given space and freedom, or any of a number of conditions that reinforce our conscious stories.

At a subconscious level, we may have conflicting desires—those that reinforce negative stories such as "I'm not worthy of being loved," "I'm a failure," "I'm wounded," "I don't fit in," or "I'm too wild, independent, sensitive, powerful, or damaged." These subconscious desires will lead us to seek out partners who reinforce these stories and then not understand why we are not happy.

A "lucid dream relationship" is what happens when we begin to awaken to the fact that no one else is actually going to be able to complete us. We still feel incomplete, but we focus on meeting our own needs rather than hoping someone else will do it for us. Of course, we still have that underlying desire to dissolve our sense of separation. We still seek to experience this dissolution in relationship. We cling to romantic fantasies that we will find the "perfect" partner or we develop a bitter and world weary attitude toward "men" or "women" or relationship in general—making them into a category. This makes us even less attractive and makes it even less likely that we will attract a partner of any sort, unless that person helps reinforce that particular story.

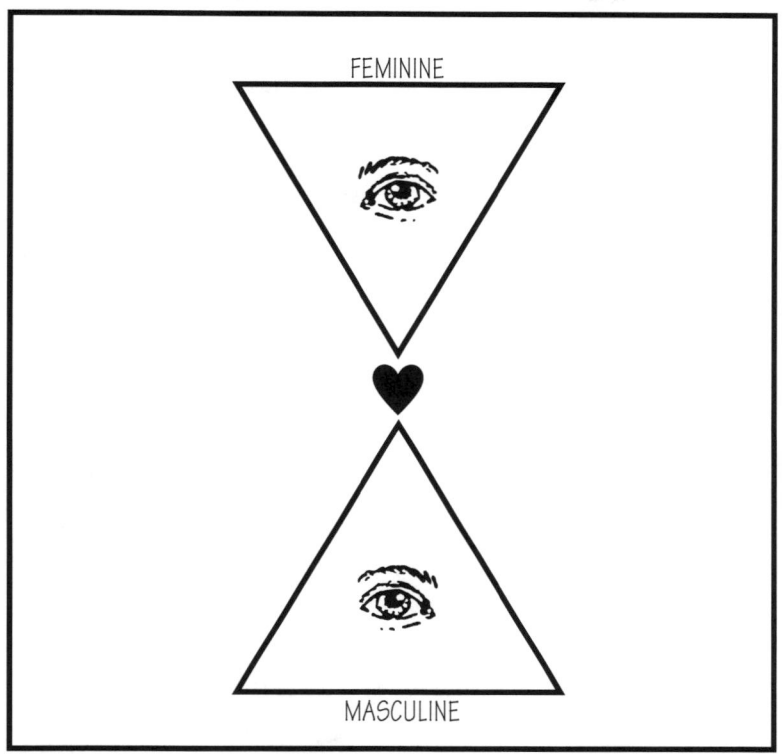

There is now a lover and a beloved.

It is only their mutual sexual attraction
that reminds them
that they are actually just complimentary aspects
of the same underlying reality,
that they are self and world,
and that they belong to each other.

Only in separation can the feminine
begin the dance of illusion.

Musings:

 Awakened relationships

*So what would an "awakened relationship" look like? An ad-
vaita couple (which may be a new oxymoron) would be a couple who were not two separate individuals, but one individual
appearing as two and making the spontaneous choice moment
-to-moment to serve each other as themselves.*

*To a lucid dreamer, this awakened relationship might look like
a throwback to a "dream relationship." We might ask how "one
individual, appearing as two" is different from a relationship in
which one is expected to complete the other? The big difference
is the starting point. If I see myself as incomplete—as needing
the other—to be filled and complete, then I am in the realm of
dream relationships.*

*If, on the other hand, I see myself as full and complete and
I recognize my fullness and completeness in another, I could
choose to commit to opening to and giving my gifts fully to this
aspect of myself that is appearing as the beloved. The difference
is that I am not seeking anything anymore. I need nothing.*

*An awakened relationship is only possible when the "need" for
relationship is transcended. This does not mean that the relationship has to end, only the "need" for it has to die. The one
who is seeking needs to die. When I awaken to the truth of
non-separation in another, that is love. I don't need love. I am
love. And if I am love, I can give love with no expectations and
no attachment to outcome. Love is not an action that I do. The
doer dies. And there are no rules. This relationship can and will
arise as passionate and erotic and friendly and deeply caring. It
is not a stereotypical "platonic" or "spiritual" relationship.*

*Love is my true nature. In an "awakened relationship," I stop
doing love and become love.*

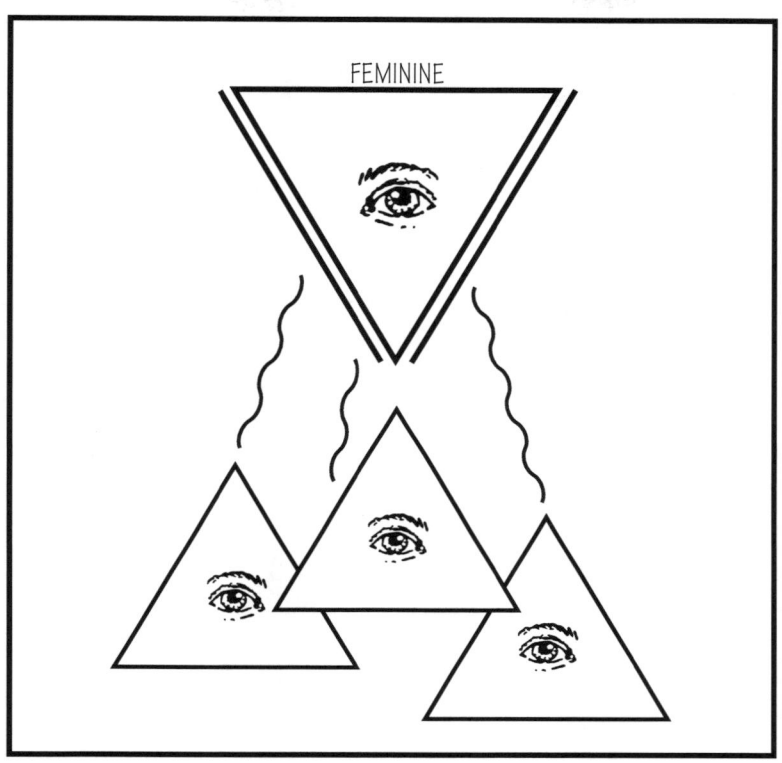

It is the feminine dance of illusion
that creates the sense
for the subjective masculine that he is not one,
but many
(remember that the subjective masculine is just
another name for the "self").

Her dance is not, strictly speaking, an illusion
but neither are the patterns
to which she gives birth "real"
in the sense of being concrete
and independent facts.

Musings:

 The paradox of desire

There is a wonderful paradox in the fact that desire takes us right up to threshold of desire-less-ness, but it can't carry us over that threshold. What we desire is to be met by the other in some kind of union. That provides the motivation to give or serve the other. Wouldn't that motivation to give be less without the promise of return? I expect that would be true—right up to the moment you cross that threshold where there is no more separation. On one side there is a giver who is giving and a doer who is doing. On the other side there is only be-ing. There is no "I" to do and no "I" to give anymore. If it looks like I am giving to the rest of the world, that is just because they still see a me that is separate from them—someone who is giving. From the other side of that threshold, it no longer feels that way.

In your life you've most likely had a lot of pleasurable moments and a lot of painful moments. Your suffering has come because the pleasurable moments did not last and you had an expectation that they should and because you have not been able to let go of the painful moments.

You've also probably had peak experiences of oneness. If you're lucky, you've had a man enter you so completely that the illusion of separation between the two of you dissolved, or you've penetrated a woman so profoundly, that the illusion of separation was immolated in the fire of passion. That gave you a taste of something you are hungry for. It has motivated you to practice hard for what you want. And what you want is to feel that feeling all the time.

The paradox is that the only way to feel that feeling all of the time is for the one who wants to feel that feeling to dissolve.

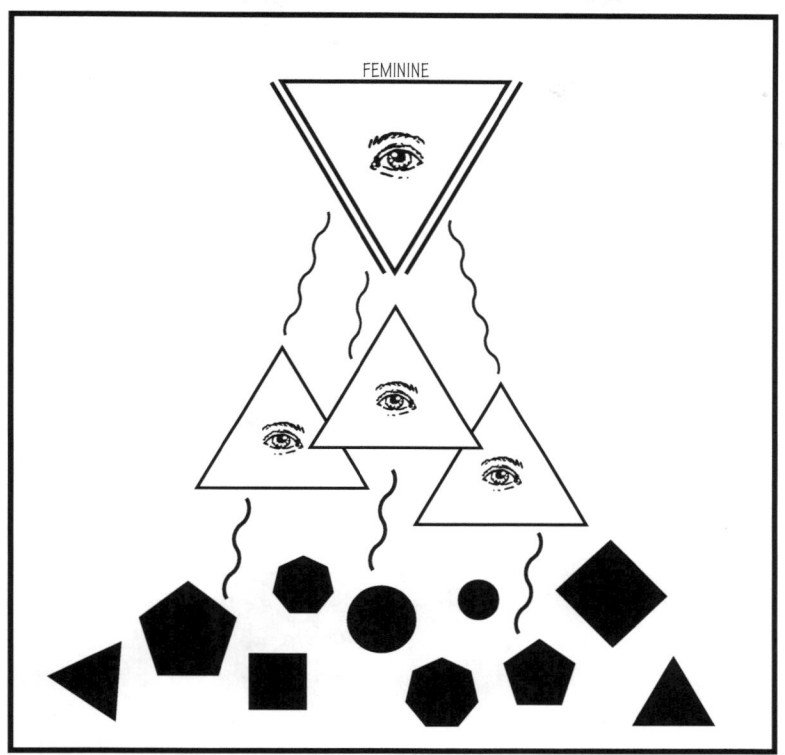

Once convinced that they are not one but many,
"subjects," or independent selves
perceive a differentiated reality.

This reality seems to be composed
of separate particles of objective fact.

And the separate selves seem to live lives
in an extended linear time.

Musings:

 Can we practice relationship?

There are skills that enhance the functionality of relationship. We can certainly become more clear and consistent as communicators, more energetically adept as lovers, and more sensitive as partners. This might be called the yoga of relationship. There is nothing wrong with perfecting the form. We can actually find a kind of temporary happiness in perfecting the form and temporary happiness is still happiness. If I was going to die tomorrow, I would prefer to die in temporary happiness rather than in unhappiness.

But form is also illusion, and illusion will only make us happy as long as it lasts. Developing energetic openness and enhanced flow is a good thing. We have these forms, so why not use them with more artfulness. It is a tragedy when people give up on the idea of wanting to open and surrender and love. This usually happens out of fear of being hurt and it leads to mediocrity and closure.

Opening or surrendering or loving with the expectation of getting anything in return (happiness, the perfect relationship, romantic magic) is still a game within a dream. In order for opening and surrendering and loving to be not something we do, but something we are, the doer as a separate being needs to dissolve.

Awakened relationship is when we convert our desire to get (more freedom or fullness, more consciousness or love) into the permanent yearning to give. And that yearning to give is permanent because it is never gratified or validated by another.

It is an arrow you shoot without needing a target.

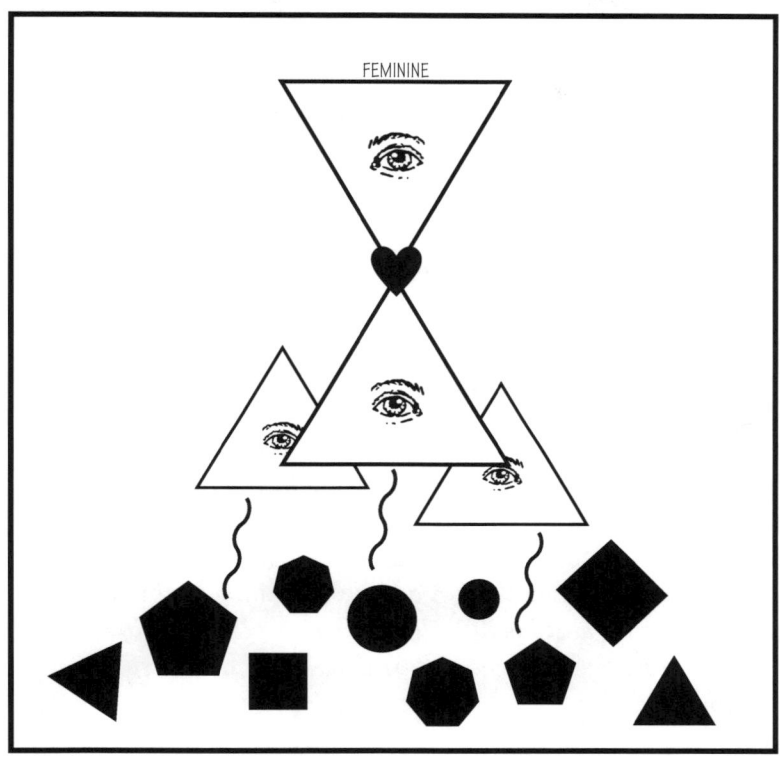

And sometimes the only memory
of unity and oneness
is to be found in the powerful attraction
of opposites.

It is as if the awareness of the underlying truth
of unity and oneness
is encoded in our DNA,
waiting to be awakened in a biological dance
of sexual intimacy that transcends
the mere need to procreate.

Musings:

 Awakened relationship for her

Basically a woman has two choices.

1. The Gentle Path: *Find a good solid man who has done some functionality or therapeutic work on his own capacity to give selflessly past his comfort zone and is willing to practice the yoga of relationship with you with the eventual goal of loving each other so transcendently that you eliminate the need for the relationship (that doesn't mean the relationship ends, just the need for it). What you are looking for in a man is that he has a strong vision of what he wants to create in the world, solid integrity and a trustable heart, a good sense of humor and resilience and a certain edginess or danger about him in at least one area of his life. He's got to be willing to do his own work and he probably has to be capable of motivating you to do your work when you don't want to. Realize that you are still seeking, but allow yourself to relax around your seeking. Observe the you that is seeking with curiosity and acceptance.*

2. The Radical Path: *Give up seeking! Stop looking for any man or any thing to fill that big hole in your life. STOP STUFFING THE HOLE! Simply start giving love and light every moment of every day no matter what you get in return or response. Stop trying to figure out what is fair and what is practical and what you deserve. Find your fullness and give everything away (or try to—because if you really find your fullness you won't be able to give it all away—it will continually refill itself). Don't make deals. Don't make plans. Live as if you are GOD's infinite water vessel. Give everyone a drink. When you have no more to give, stop giving and sit still until you find your way back to your fullness.*

And in that dance,
the more polarized the partners are—
the more they manifest complimentary
rather than similar qualities—
the stronger the attraction will be.

And the stronger the attraction,
the greater the possibility that
through relationship and sexual intimacy
the world of separate forms
and identities will dissolve
in the bliss of union.

Musings:

 Awakened relationship for him

Basically a man has two choices.

1. The Gentle Path: *Find a woman with a heart glow about her who has done some functionality or therapeutic work on her own capacity to give selflessly past her comfort zone and is willing to practice the yoga of relationship with you with the eventual goal of loving each other so transcendently that you eliminate the need for the relationship (that doesn't mean the relationship ends, just the need for it). What you are looking for in a woman is that she has a strong love of life in all its forms, a desire to shine the full spectrum of the light that is inside her (not just a few colors, but all of them), a capacity to feel her feelings and let them go without overly identifying with them and a willingness to surrender open as love in at least some aspects of your relationship together. Realize that you are still seeking, but allow yourself to relax around your seeking. Observe the you that is seeking with curiosity and acceptance.*

2. The Radical Path: *Give up seeking! Stop looking for any woman or any thing to fill that big hole in your life. STOP STUFFING THE HOLE! Simply start living your mission— giving your gift of consciousness, presence, and depth every moment of every day no matter what you get in return or response. If you don't really know what your mission is, put everything else on hold until you figure that out. Don't make deals. Don't make plans. Live as if you are intimate with death. Know what your gifts are and try to give them away every day, so that if you die in your sleep, you will die empty.*

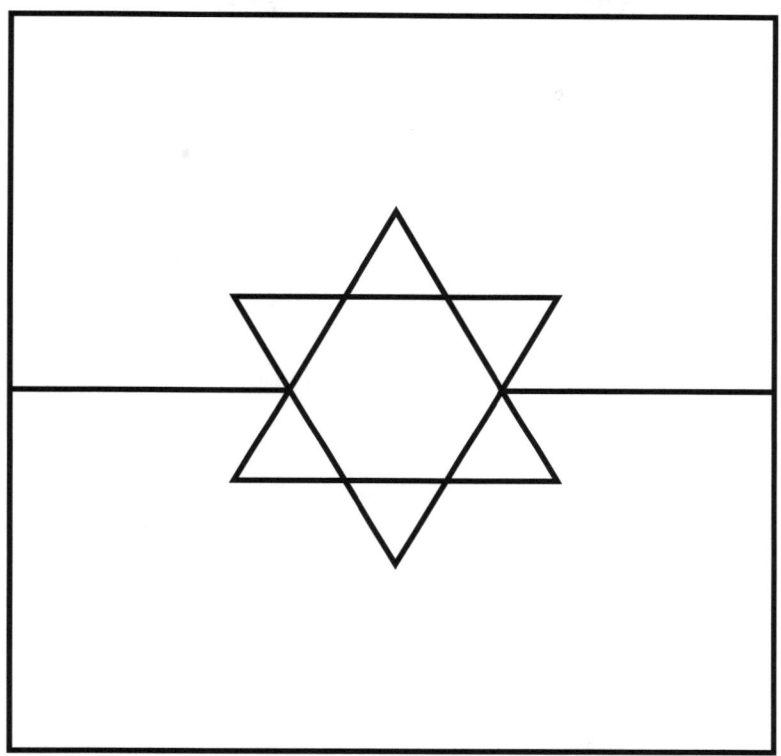

Of course, it doesn't last...

But it offers a sweet drop of nectar,
the taste and scent of something long forgotten.

Musings:

 All you are is love

In most spiritual traditions, desire is a destructive force. We are taught to reduce or eliminate desire in order to eliminate suffering. But the real problem is not the desire, it is that we objectify desire and assume that our suffering is caused by the absence of the object of our desire.

It doesn't matter what we desire. There is no good or bad. But when an object or person or state becomes the focus of our desire, it reduces us. It constricts the amount of energy, consciousness, and light that can flow through us and we live shallow lives of constant suffering. We suffer because we do not have the object of our desire and we suffer because we get the object of our desire and we are still unhappy.

We are all born into this realm of desire. We find ourselves here, pursuing our desires with abandon. This is not a bad thing. It can be intoxicating and even addicting, but it is important to remember that we cannot both pursue desire and awaken to the realization that we are desire at the same time.

Our practice then is neither to sharpen our desires by obsessive focus nor to act as if we had no desires, but rather to act as if all of our desires were constantly being met in each and every moment. Whether you call this surrendering to or awakening to our true nature as desire, it is one of the most powerful practices.

"*Separation is the absence of love,*
        and love is the absence of separation."

Ramesh Balsekar

The Yoga of relationship
is the refinement of energetic sensitivity
and the cultivation of attraction.

The Dharma of relationship
is the recognition that the beloved
is not a long-lost half,
not a soul-mate separated at birth,
not, in fact, an "other" at all.

The beloved is the "me" I see in the mirror
after the mirror dissolves away.

Chapter Six
Bliss Dreaming

When we dream,
images arise as the dialog between the nondual
nature of source consciousness and the separate
ego-self we habitually perceive ourselves to be in
the waking world.
As we move deeper, all the images fall away and we
return to our true nature as Bliss.

When Bliss dreams,
the world we refer to as the waking world
blooms into existence.
Our challenge is to become lucid
in the realm that Bliss is dreaming. Learning to live,
love, and serve in wakeful awareness
is the challenge.

Musings:

 The beginning of the world

The world began this morning at 6:28 AM—much as it does every day—to the pale green glow of the clock beside my bed.

Actually it began sometime earlier as that Bliss that is dreaming me contracted and coagulated into a form and identity that I believe I recall from the day before and the day before that in a seamlessly perfect illusion.

It feels like I have been here all along.

I've been involved in dream work for nearly 30 years. I've probably learned more about nonduality from the study and play with my dreams and the dreams of clients than from any other source.

I used to have these dreams
of being chased by terrifying things
that wanted to kill me.

They would chase me
through elaborate landscapes.

They would kill people I loved.
I would fight them off, but there were always more,
regardless of how many I killed.

There was nothing I could do but run and hide.

But they would always find me.

Musings:

 The beginning of the world redux

The world began again this morning at 6:28 AM—much as it does every day—to the pale green glow of the clock beside my bed.

It is really weird how convincing this illusion of time passing is. I have no real proof that this isn't the first day of my life. I have no objective evidence for an existence extending backward into time. What I have is a consensual agreement that this is how things work.

What keeps me from seeing the beauty of the woman I wake up beside each morning? Only the sense that I have seen her face thousands of times before. What makes this illusion so convincing is that I seem to wake in the middle of an ongoing drama. But that is exactly what makes my dreams so convincing—that I wake into a world in the middle of an ongoing drama.

I felt helpless, powerless, afraid, alone.

Always at the last moment,
I would wrench myself from the dream,
as if too long underwater,
clawing my way to the surface
for air.

I would wake up in a cold sweat, panting,
feeling my heart pounding,
struggling to reassure myself
that I was safe.

Musings:

 The cycle of consciousness

Nondual awareness is not nearly as foreign as it might seem at first. Every twenty-four hours we cycle from waking into dreaming into deep dreamless sleep, into the nondual awareness of oneness and then back again through deep dreamless sleep, the dreaming, and into waking. We fall asleep and we fall awake. We relax and dissolve past the solid into the shimmering and transient into the emptiness and then we contract and coagulate back into form.

I have come to believe that one of the most useful and profound perspectives for dream work is to see it as the dialogue between the contracted egoic sense of self that we habitually experience as our waking selves and the expanded sense of the divine or undifferentiated consciousness. This dialogue is played out on the stage of an infinitely diverse and changing landscape populated with all the things that we cling to.

This dialogue occurs as me seeing myself as solid, separate, and unique in a realm in which that sense is going to be continually challenged and frustrated. The extent to which I am able to relax into the impermanence and transience of phenomenon in this realm is the extent to which I experience this realm as peaceful, beautiful and joyful. The extent to which I constrict and resist this transience, is the extent to which my dreams (my reality) become frightening, frustrating, and anxiety provoking.

If only I could consistently remember this.

I sought help for these recurring nightmares.

I learned where they came from.

I understood them
as well and as deeply as I could.

And still they came to me.

I could not awaken to the dream
from within the dream.

I was a prisoner of the dream.

Musings:

 Reality/relativity

I dream that Albert Einstein is writing a formula on a blackboard with white chalk. He writes "R – pR = E". He explains that "R" stands for reality and "pR" represents what we think reality should be. When the difference between the two is great, the energy we are losing "E" on a daily basis around a specific issue is high. He adds that most of us spend our depleted energy continually trying to change "R" (reality) rather than reevaluating "pR" (our sense of what reality should be). We should, he further explains, always work to ensure the highest functional level of energy first, because this is where the power to influence the world of form and appearances comes from.

After years of dream work, my own and with others, I have increasingly come to appreciate a way of approaching the world that looks to observe and describe first, without jumping to interpretation and the assignment of meaning or significance.

In dream work, the first question we ask of an image that arises in our waking or dreaming worlds is "What is it?" What is it in itself? What is its nature? How is it different or distinctive from something similar? Instead of asking what it means, instead of judging or evaluating first, we need to return to a way of looking that is open to a full range of possibilities.

As in my dream of Albert Einstein, I often find that when things annoy and irritate me, I need to first ask what is it that is actually happening. My irritation usually grows from my sense that something different should be happening. When I bring what I think should be happening into alignment with what actually is happening without attaching meaning or making assumptions, I find that I have more energy and a clearer picture of my circumstances.

When I awoke from these nightmares
I did everything in my power
to tell myself that I was no longer
in the dream.

I reassured myself that all was well.
I got out of bed and walked around.
I drank a glass of water.
I turned lights on.
I denied that other world.

It was not real.
It was not me.

Musings:

 Inquiry and dream work

Another precious jewel we mine from the practice of Dream Yoga is the idea of inquiry or what is called a phenomenological approach. The best dream work does not come from dictionaries of symbols and symbolic meaning. It does not come from attaching stories to our dreams too quickly.

The best dream work asks the simple questions "what is it" and "what does it want." Dreamers are often anxious to attach meaning to their dreams—fixing them or pinning them to boards like specimens of beautiful and exotic butterflies. Once pinned and named, we believe we have regained control over them. But all we have done is remove the magic and the life and the mystery from them.

In working with clients and students, I have discovered that even when they don't remember their dreams, their waking experiences, when treated as dreams, can be revealing and transformative. By bringing the same approach of inquiry to the waking experiences that one might bring to a dream, we open the experience without robbing it of its life and mystery.

I will often ask the same kinds of questions of a dreamer that a Zen master might ask of a student. By continually asking what is it and what is it beneath that and what is it beneath that, we create a rich canvas of possibility. I will often end a session without a fixed meaning and ask the dreamer to just be with the menu of possibilities without fixing on any one.

Then one night I awoke differently.

I was paralyzed.
I could not move.
I could not get out of bed.
I could not speak.

All sorts of thoughts went through my head.
Am I having a stroke?
Am I dying?

Am I still dreaming?

Musings:

 The taste of impermanence

If you spend much time reflecting on the laws that seem to operate in the dreaming realm, you will notice that things do not stay the same. Things do not cling to their form. A car you are driving becomes a bike you are riding. An escalator becomes a mountain path or an amusement park ride. A person you know remains the person you know, while their outward appearance becomes completely foreign to you. You can be plummeting to Earth one moment and then defying the laws of gravity the next. You can start out in Hoboken and cross a bridge into Hong Kong. You are yourself as a child and an old woman at the same time.

In the yoga of (or spiritual practice of working with) dreams we uncover these naturally occurring pointing-out instructions to the nature of impermanence and nonduality. In dreams, things start out appearing to be either this or that and invariably end up being this and that.

It is a very useful practice to recapture the lack of resistance we tend to have to this realm of shifting and impermanence and apply it to our waking world. While we might find ourselves caught off guard by the sudden shift from one thing to another in a dream, we usually just accept the new reality, integrating it seamlessly into a new paradigm of reality. In the dreaming, we don't stop the game. We don't say "no, this is unacceptable— this is not the way it is supposed to be." We integrate what is arising in the "now" and move forward.

What if we could live that kind of "Yes" in the realm we call waking? What if we could live more fully in the now of what is actually arising?

I wanted to reassure myself
that now I was awake and I was not dreaming,
just like I usually did,
but I could not figure out how.

This was even more disturbing.
I was not feeling better.

And then something came to me.

I could not run away from the feelings
so I ran toward them.

Musings:

 ## Caught on the wheel

More common than nightmares, or dreams that trigger fear, are dreams that trigger anxiety or frustration. I believe that anxiety dreams reflect the ambivalence or fragility we feel around our own identities. In dreams we often find ourselves caught halfway between the perspective that we <u>are</u> our egoic, contracted and separate selves and the deeper awareness that we are something more than that. Anxiety dreams (like being back in school, unprepared for a test, naked) are all about how we are seen by others. When we are clinging to an identity in waking life, especially when the solidity and permanence of that identity has already begun to come undone, the dreamer (or Dream-maker as Arnold Mindell identifies this aspect of the mystery) offers us anxiety plays. Those on a spiritual path who begin to really integrate the significance of nondual awareness often go through a period in which these anxiety dreams are amplified.

Frustration dreams usually signal another form of egoic stuckness. Frustration dreams usually involve being lost or losing important things, or being unable to find a particular person, place, or thing that we just turned our back on for a moment. Frustration dreams sometimes also involve impossible tasks like packing a simple suitcase for a trip and realizing that you have far more to take than could ever fit in this bag. Frustration dreams are also often about being late for important events or connections, which can bleed into anxiety dreams when we begin to worry about how we will be perceived if we are late.

Interestingly enough, frustration dreams like this are common to people who are beginning to do mindfulness practice and who realize just how frustrating and out-of-control their habitual mind chatter actually is.

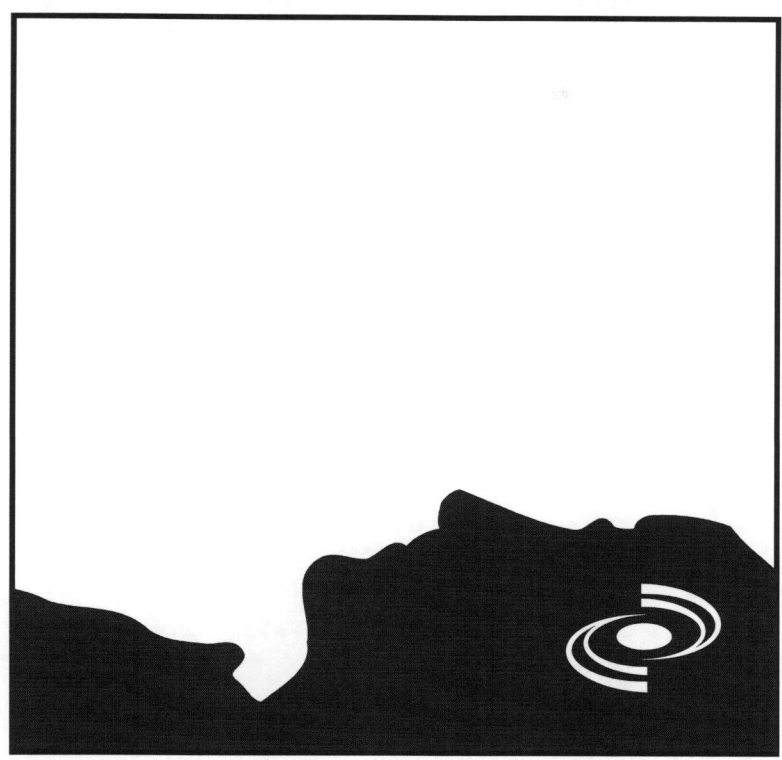

I just stayed with the sensations in my body.

I reentered the dreamscape
with consciousness.

I recalled the things that seemed so real and so
separate from me and I told myself that all of it,
every frightening detail, came from me. It was my
dream. It was, in fact, not separate from me at all.

It was me chasing me.
It was me wanting to kill me.
It was me frightening me.

Musings:

 Impersonation (from my dream journal)

I have perfected this impersonation.

I do me better than anyone else I know.

I can, in fact, pass for me at almost any moment.

People say they cannot tell the difference between me and me doing me.

I catch glimpses of myself in mirrors and I find that I cannot tell the difference either.

When I am awake, I am on stage, doing my impersonation.

When I slip past dreams into that place where there is only me, I relax.

We usually have some sense of an "I" in a dream, either as an actor or as an observer, but dream work teaches us that the distinction between the "I" of the dream and all the other characters and all the other elements of the dream (objects, animals, landscapes, phenomena) is an illusion. It is all the dreamer. What else could there be?

The "I" of the dream with which the dreamer identifies has opinions about the others in the dream and thoughts and feelings about what is happening in the dream, but these serve the primary purpose of reinforcing the identity of the dreamer.

It is the same when we wake from our night dreams into our day dreams.

I stayed with the fear,
the shortness of breath, the paralysis, the panic,
the anxiety, the pounding heart.

And watched them dissolve
in the solvent of awareness.

I had created all of this
out of nothing,
out of the play of stillness and vibration.

And, no matter how solid and real it seemed,
I knew there was only me.

Musings:

 Integrating the dream state

When you wake from a dream that is frightening or big and dramatic, especially one that has triggered strong emotions, the tendency is to get up and move around and literally "shake off" the feelings of the dream.

Resist this urge. Remain in the position in which you came awake. Reenter the dream and remember it in as much detail as possible while simultaneously holding the sense that every realistic detail of the dream, every brick and stone, every fierce creature or frightening ghost, every drop of that tsunami and every sensation you experienced all came from you. This is you scaring you. This is you challenging you. This is you creating situations and circumstances to call your attention to what is blocking you from embracing the truth of reality—that we are all one.

Stay with this experience of being fully present with the lingering emotions and felt bodily sensations from the dream and also embrace the witness that is aware that the whole experience is simply illusion.

As you move through your day, take short breaks (micropractices) to recall this simultaneous awareness of being both the dream and the dreamer at the same time. Allow yourself to be both the dream and the dreamer in your waking experience.

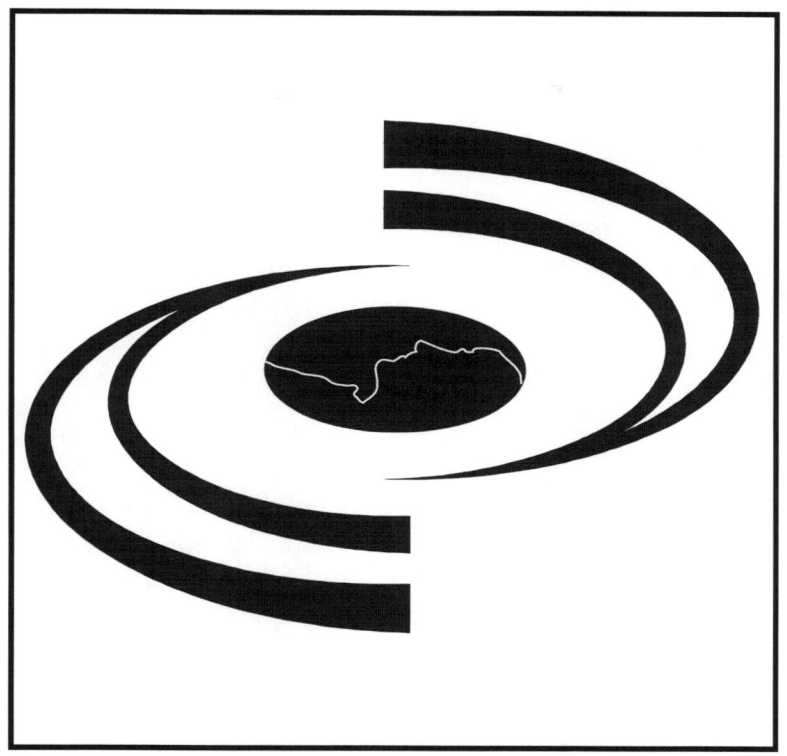

I felt like GOD,
but not as an egoic, all-powerful, deity.

I felt like the knowing of GOD,
the suchness of GOD.

I had dreamed this dream to know myself.
I had dreamed this dream to
experience some aspect of myself.

Fleeing from the dream, denying the dream,
was denying myself and denying GOD.

Musings:

 Night karma.

The world ends a little after 11:48 PM—at least that is the last time I remember seeing the soft glow of the clock by my bed.

I reach out and touch my wife's sleeping body. She is already gone, or, more appropriately, I am already gone to her. The dog on its cushion sighs and then it is gone as well.

As I relax—as the "me" dissolves—I slowly stop maintaining the illusion of separation. I stop creating the sound of cars on the street, the hum of air conditioning, the soft purr of my wife's breathing. I stop creating the mattress beneath me, the blanket on top of me, the roof over my head. Who I think I am and what I think I feel fades.

In its place, for a time, are even more fantastic and malleable inventions, landscapes, individuals and experiences. But those will fade as well, until there is nothing left.

It is the end of the world as I know it. I am dying, but I feel no panic at it all going away. Perhaps it is because I have comforted myself by planting the seed that I will be back, it will all come back, just as I've left it.

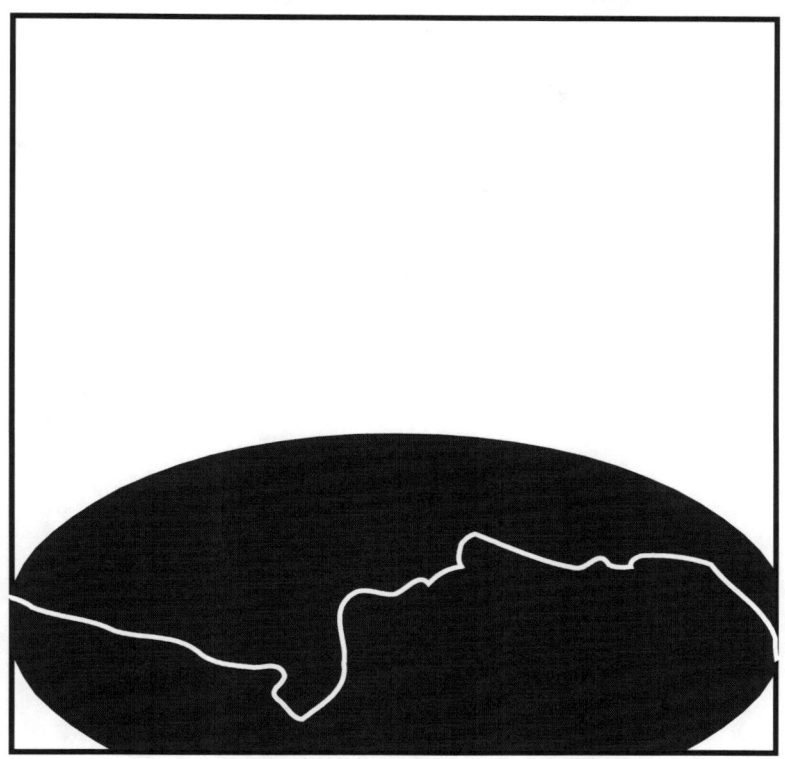

And with that,
I stopped having these dreams.

But, I have never lost the sensation
that I might be dreaming right now.

I have clever tests for whether I am dreaming
or whether I am being dreamed,
but nothing can tell me with certainty
that this is not a dream.

I once thought that one would go mad
living like that.

Chapter Seven
Just This Side of Enlightenment

As useful as it is to understand
what nondual awareness is,
it can be equally useful
to understand what it isn't.

It also helps to recognize when understanding
a little bit about nondual awareness
is a dangerous thing.

Musings:

 Who let the dog-ma out?

When we hear the word dogma, most of us think of political or religiously imposed truths that we are not supposed to question, but there is another dogma that is far more insidious.

Dogma means a principle or set of principles laid down by an authority as incontrovertibly true. If you are closing in on what the truth of pure awareness is, there is a terrifying identity challenge underway. If you are not feeling it, then you are not as close as you think you are.

You may be resisting it (My old identity is just fine, thank you. I see what happens when people start to get shaken loose from their identity and I'm not interested), fantasizing that you can control it (I'm not going to let go of my old identity until I have a firm grasp on the new identity), or imagining that you have already experienced it and are on the other side of it (I'm free and no longer attached to my old identity).

You will not come to enlightenment without an identity death. One of the signs of an authentic spiritual identity crisis is that we either let our dogma out or it escapes and we have to deal with defending it. Our personal dogma—our ego dogma—is that set of beliefs we have about the world that must not be questioned. When jobs and relationships and prosperity and comfort and health all get yanked out from under our feet, we still cling to our dogma. It is usually the last thing to go and yet it is the thing that most interferes with our awakening. The reason that it is so hard to let go of our dogma is that our dogma directly props up the dictatorship of the "I." It is what our ego is insisting is absolutely true about us and about how we see the world. It must not be questioned, because it gives us the only remaining stability we think we have.

Beware of getting stuck
somewhere between
being sanctimonious and self-absorbed
and simply replacing one artificial identity
with another.

"I used to be a material seeker
and then I was a spiritual seeker
and now I am beyond seeking."

Maybe,
or maybe you just have a new
"enlightened" name tag.

Musings:

 Recognizing dog-ma

- *If you think your preferences are facts, that's your dogma.*

- *If you are convinced that you are an introvert or an extrovert or (substitute any convenient psychological label), that's your dogma.*

- *If you think an archetype or an astrological sign is what you are, rather than a momentary expression of your energy, that's your dogma.*

- *If you think you have the way the world works figured out, that's your dogma.*

- *If you see the world as a cruel and violent place where most people are lower on the evolutionary ladder than you, that's your dogma.*

- *If you see the world as being filled with betrayers and abusers and you are either the universal suffering victim or the avenging angel of justice, or both, that's your dogma.*

- *If you see the world as being filled with special people who get it and are close to the divine and you still don't get it and aren't close to the divine, that's your dogma.*

- *If you see the world as a Zen utopia where everything that happens is perfect and for the best, that's your dogma.*

- *If you think you have the good guys and the bad guys figured out, that's your dogma.*

- *If you think that you need what you need in order to be happy, that's your dogma.*

Buddhism was founded in the idea
that some people would devote their lives
to seeking or living enlightenment
for the benefit of all sentient beings.

Buddhist monks depend on the charity of others.
They manage to do this without suggesting that
their benefactors are deluded.

Perhaps they just have better manners.

Musings:

 A walk in the dog-ma park

Our egoic dogma is not so different from the "spiritual" truths of the Catholic Church. Catholic dogma insists upon the infallibility of the Pope in the same way that our personal dogma insists upon the infallibility of the "I."

A good spiritual fire (one that might actually transform you) is going to challenge your dogma and it won't be comfortable. If there is a dogma that you are willing to easily give up, it isn't dogma for you any longer. It is something that you have already released but that you keep around for just such occasions, so that you can toss the spiritual fire a hunk of wood without it costing you anything.

The best place to find your egoic edge is when you are "doggedly" defending a preference as a "fact" or a point of view as the "truth." You may have lots of "anecdotal and statistical evidence" to back up your dogma. You may have lots of life experience confirming your dogma as unassailable truth, but it is still just dogma. It is the sum total of the thoughts and feelings you have collected in order to build an identity. It is not who you are, and more important than that, it is suppressing who you really are. It is hiding who you really are behind a protective wall or mask.

If you are drawn to the idea of enlightenment or pure awareness or in some way, shape, or form, you want to serve love and consciousness more. You will need to stop spending your energy—your life force—in suffering. That doesn't mean experiencing no pain or being artificially blissful. It means to opt out of as much suffering as possible and to do that you have to become more conscious and more compassionate and your personal dogma will do nothing but get in the way of that.

It seems odd
to have to point out the absurdity of the
"I'm more nondual than you are"
position.

I know it feels that way right now,
but the superiority you are feeling
is just another flavor of the
separation you are convinced you've overcome.

When you feel uplifted and humbled
in the same breath, call me.

Musings:

 Dog-ma spotting

While a teacher is not essential to awakening into pure aware-ness, one of the ways a good teacher can help you is by pointing out when your dogma is on the loose. A good teacher will not really be interested in replacing it with new dogma, only in bringing consciousness to the illusory nature of that dogma.

Of course, you won't like hearing that what you believe to be true, may not be either true or useful. None of us like to be challenged in that way, but it serves us to be attuned to the fact that when we feel our dogma straining against the choke chain—when we feel ourselves digging in our heels and insist-ing that our dogma is an accurate picture of reality—it is a good time to slow down and reflect instead of reactively de-fending our position.

It is an interesting phenomenon that from one side of awaken-ing our ideas about how the world works and what our egos need easily become dogma. On the other side of awakening we may still have ideas about how the world works and we may still have preferences, but we are not attached to them being real any longer. They are ideas with which we play lightly and sometimes passionately, but they are simply no longer dogma. They do not cause us to suffer because we are no longer in-vested in them being true.

It would be nice if awakening
helped one become
less stupid,
less rude,
less annoying,
and generally less insensitive
to the suffering of others,
but maybe that is asking
for too much.

Musings:

 The gravity of illusion

There are all sorts of thought games we could play with the relationship between apparent forms and underlying unity. Quantum physicists tell us that atoms and their component parts are largely just empty space. In fact, there is so much space that one wonders why forms don't just interpenetrate one another.

But the fact is that as forms, we don't, or we don't appear to, or when we do, there are consequences that seem rather extreme from the perspective of surviving in this current form. Two waves made of the same underlying stuff—water—can crash together in a way that seems to annihilate one. They can crash together in a way that seems to dissipate both. They can cross each other in a way that creates an interference pattern or a new third wave. But at some level we understand that despite appearances, the underlying "oceanness" is in tact. It is in tact as "no wave" or "new wave." What seemed separate and distinct a moment ago is once again a oneness.

The ultimate attachment, of course, is to life in the form we appear to be taking right now. Ultimately, we come back up against the mystery. We can speculate, but we do not know what, other than GOD, persists beyond the death of the physical form we have taken in this incarnation.

There are physical laws that "seem" to operate in this realm. No amount of enlightenment or wishful thinking seems able to bypass the appearance of those laws. Perhaps there are parallel realms in which those laws do not apply. Perhaps we will one day transcend the need to have these physical laws appear at all. But I think that if pure awareness truly shifts our perspective, it is in the direction of the appreciation and embrace of what arises rather than the rejection and negation of it.

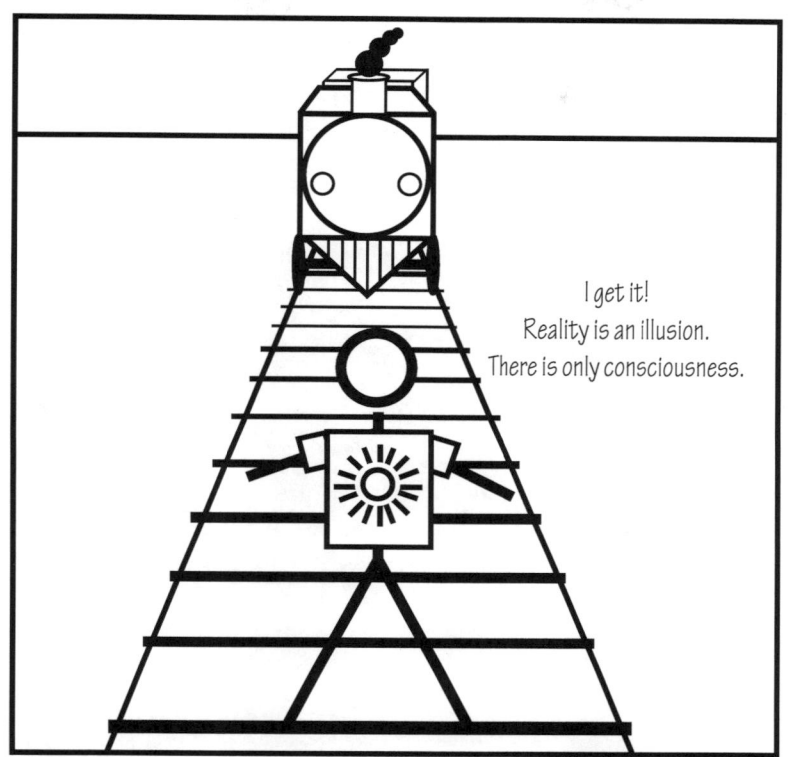

Have you ever noticed how
a little spiritual truth
can be a dangerous thing?

It's kind of like GOD's game
of rock-paper-scisssors.

Yeah, we know this is all just a hand
taking different forms,
but scissors still beats paper
and paper still beats rock
and rock still beats scissors
in this game.

Chapter Eight
The Other Side of Enlightenment

In the film *God and the Buddha,* with Robert Thurman, Deepak Chopra recounts a conversation with the Dalai Lama in which Chopra was holding forth eloquently with an abstract notion of spirit and consciousness when the Dalai Lama politely interrupted him and asked "But how does this change a person's life?"

This is the essence of why I wrote this book. I, like Deepak Chopra, can revel in the most abstract of spiritual theories, but, in the end, enlightenment must mean an end to the suffering caused by separation. This isn't a self-help project. It isn't another rearrangement of the same old furniture. On the other side of awakening, what is life like?

Musings:

 A life of saying yes

What does it feel like to live in the state of pure awareness?

The art form of improvisational theatre is based on two simple premises. The first is saying yes to whatever arises. As long as a player figures out how to say yes to what arises, the play continues and has a life of its own. That life includes the actors who are simultaneously aware that they are acting and playing their roles completely. They don't identify with any particular part because they understand that the parts are not them, they are not the parts, and everything can and will change in an instant. Clinging to any particular identity in this game creates instant suffering.

Each of us has a script in our heads and in that script there is a part for a "me" and multiple "you" roles for others to play. This script is so entangled with our life experience that we come to believe we are the "me" characters in our plays. We spend most of our lives running around trying to cast others in the "you" roles, expecting them to play the parts we have written. Unfortunately, they have their own scripts and are trying to produce their own plays and because they aren't playing their roles as written, the play doesn't go as we would like and we suffer.

Enlightenment is not refusing to play. It is letting go of the script and the "me" role and choosing to play at improvisation.

The second premise of successful improvisation is the offering. A good player offers the most creative and inviting lines. A good player is generous. A good player is always setting others up to succeed. When we do not have a separate and unique "me" to defend, our lives become about generous offerings.

Enlightenment is when your focus shifts from what you can get to the quality of your offerings.

Abiding in nondual or pure awareness
is not a means to an end,
but neither is it an end in itself.

In the sleepwalk of duality there is a mountain.

In awakening to the truth of nonduality
there is no mountain.

Beyond awakening, there is,
once again, a mountain.

Musings:

 And it's all about the offering

If we live the truth, that everything arises out of GOD or core consciousness, then the illusion of separate things gives way to the perception of GOD's offerings.

There is no keyboard in front of me. There is only GOD "keyboarding." There is no chair beneath me, there is only GOD "chairing." There is no dog lying at my feet, there is only GOD "dogging." There is no woman padding about the winter house with her laughter and her affection, there is only GOD "womaning." There is no me struggling to find words to describe an ineffable sensation, there is only GOD making a "me-shaped" offering in the form of a book to GOD.

There is no me perceiving. There is only perception arising. GOD tosses a ball. GOD catches the ball. I still feel as if perception is going on. I even feel at times as if there is a me that is perceiving, but I don't cling to either the perceptions or the character that appears to be me perceiving.

These are GOD's offerings. For a reason I cannot comprehend, GOD dreamed up a "me" to play in and bear witness to this great game of improvisation. GOD is the ultimate improv player. Every day I seem to wake up in a world that has been carefully and perfectly designed for the play ahead of me that day. The trees and the sun and the tea and the toast and the dog that appears to need a walk and the woman I seem to love, all warm and steamy from the shower—they all arise in perfect order and with impeccable timing.

Like Marlon Brando as Vito Corleone in "The Godfather," GOD is constantly making offers "I" cannot refuse.

If you have to avoid form
in order to avoid getting lost in form
you're probably not as awake as you think are.

There are no rules for this,
no way you are supposed to be,
no "you" to be any particular way.

But, on the other side of enlightenment,
GOD seems to offer qualities
that might be picked up like useful tools,
not claimed, owned, or used to build some new
identity, but set aside gently at the end of the day.

Musings

 Compassion Arises

There seems to be this idea that enlightenment or pure aware-
ness means no longer feeling things. This arises from the idea
that on the other side of enlightenment there is no longer a per-
son to feel things. This is not the case. You do not disappear, the
"you" disappears. The illusory construct that you believed was
"you" is what dissolves, but even then it seldom dissolves com-
pletely or all at once. That "you" was like a transparent shield
that you held up when you encountered other "you" identities
and they were holding up their "you" shields as well.

Without your shield, there is only what shows up, what arises.
There is nothing between you and GOD now. There is nothing
between you and all GOD's offerings. Walking down a crowd-
ed street, you meet GOD and GOD and GOD and GOD and
sometimes GOD makes laughter erupt and sometimes GOD
makes tears flow, but the GOD that arises in the you that is
laughing and crying is true compassion.

On the other side of enlightenment, you still feel, in fact, you
feel more intensely. You feel what arises naturally and you al-
low what arises to subside. There is a you that feels but not a
you that collects feelings, clings to feelings, editorializes feelings,
judges feelings. They are like weather. It is raining until it isn't
raining anymore and no amount of wanting the rain to be over
or wanting the rain to last will make any difference.

When you wake from the dream and walk down that crowded
street it doesn't matter whether you see GOD in every face or
yourself in every face. What naturally arises is nameless com-
passion. Loving without expectation.

"The key to compassion is that it is more fun."

Robert Thurman

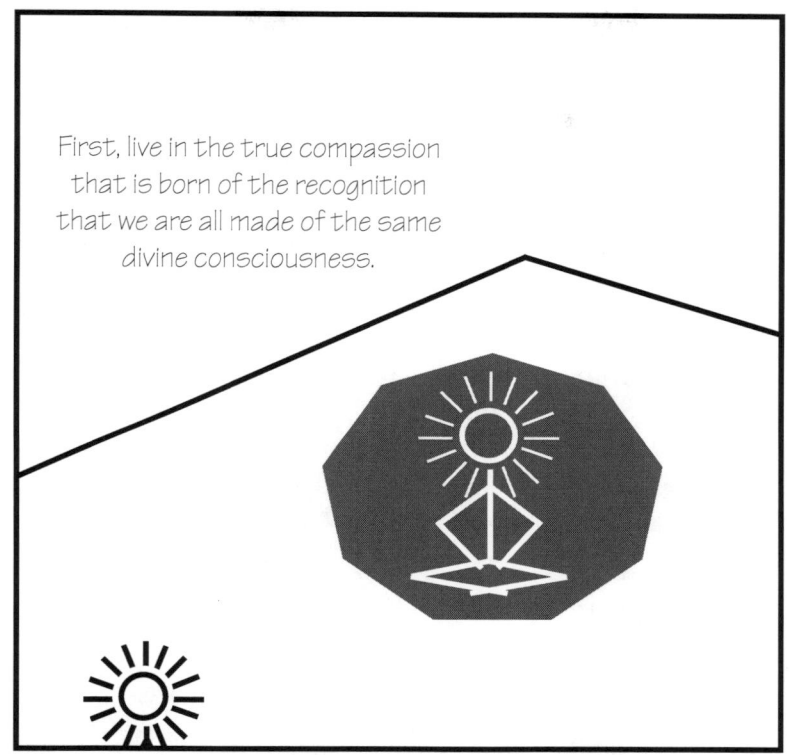

First, live in the true compassion
that is born of the recognition
that we are all made of the same
divine consciousness.

Compassion.

To allow even one drop of pure awareness
to rest on your tongue
is enough to awaken you
to the only genuine response to the
birthing and blissing and suffering and dying
that is life in this realm.

When there is no separation
we can do no better
than to love our neighbors as ourselves.

We can do no better than to live as compassion.

Musings

 Curiosity arises

As with feelings, there is a common idea that on the other side of enlightenment, there are no thoughts. It is absurd to equate the lack of thoughts with enlightenment. If that were the case we would be enlightened every time we fell into deep sleep. This idea probably grows from the meditative practices that aim at stilling the over-active mind. But the real practice of meditation is not about eliminating thoughts, it is about standing aside from them, refusing to identify with them, placing them back in their proper place.

In pure awareness, there are still thoughts. Thoughts still arise. What is missing is that there is no one collecting those thoughts in order to build an identity. In meditation we learn to watch the thoughts that arise and move across our internal landscapes without having our attention leashed to those thoughts. We understand that those thoughts are not who we are.

Because thoughts and feelings will continue to arise even after you awaken from the dream, the best tool to pick up is that of curiosity. Observe that thought arising for the wonder that it is. You need not either discount it or embrace it. It is just a thought. Follow it with curiosity if you choose, but don't cling to it, don't defend it.

Curiosity means really looking, really seeing what is here right now. Before awakening we don't attend to what is here right now because we are consumed with some memory of the past or fantasy about the future. After awakening we pick up time as a kind of useful tool and then set it aside when we are done. After awakening we are endlessly curious about what is arising in this moment.

Acknowledge the mystery
—that ultimately—
you don't know.
Then meet that mystery with curiosity.

Curiosity.
You will find yourself getting lost in form.
You will find these old patterns of closure
reemerging.

It is foolish to waste energy berating yourself.

Simply observe yourself with curiosity.

And when GOD shows up at 3:00 AM
and wants to talk to you about your death,
serve your oldest scotch
in your finest glass
with wonder, awe, and humility.

Musings

 Creativity arises

"Every time I open my eyes,
  I invite the world to take shape,
  and every time the world takes shape,
  I am invited to open my eyes."

Rupert Spira
"The Unknowable Reality of Things"

If the world is perfect as it is, then why make anything? Why create. I'm glad this question has not plagued Rupert Spira. Being an eloquent voice for nondual awareness has not stopped him from creating breathtakingly beautiful ceramic art.

The real experience of enlightenment is one of immediacy and aliveness, not inertia. The world becomes a wonder that takes, shape every time we open our eyes. If that aliveness wants to express itself through you as abiding in stillness and meditative equanimity, that's beautiful. If that aliveness wants to express itself through you as devotional prayer and ceremony and acts the world identifies as being spiritual, that is beautiful too. If that vital sense of aliveness wants to express itself through meaningful work and intimate relationship, then let that be as well.

GOD, or love, or consciousness is the ultimate creative force. We don't know <u>why</u> GOD chooses to create—to dream form out of emptiness—but creation seems to be GOD's vibration in this realm. If we are GOD, then it seems as though it might be natural that we would want to express the aliveness and immediacy of the unfolding world creatively as art, music, poetry, dance or any creative endeavor. Not to cling to an identity as an "artist," but to allow GOD to work through us to express beauty or truth as temporary forms in this realm.

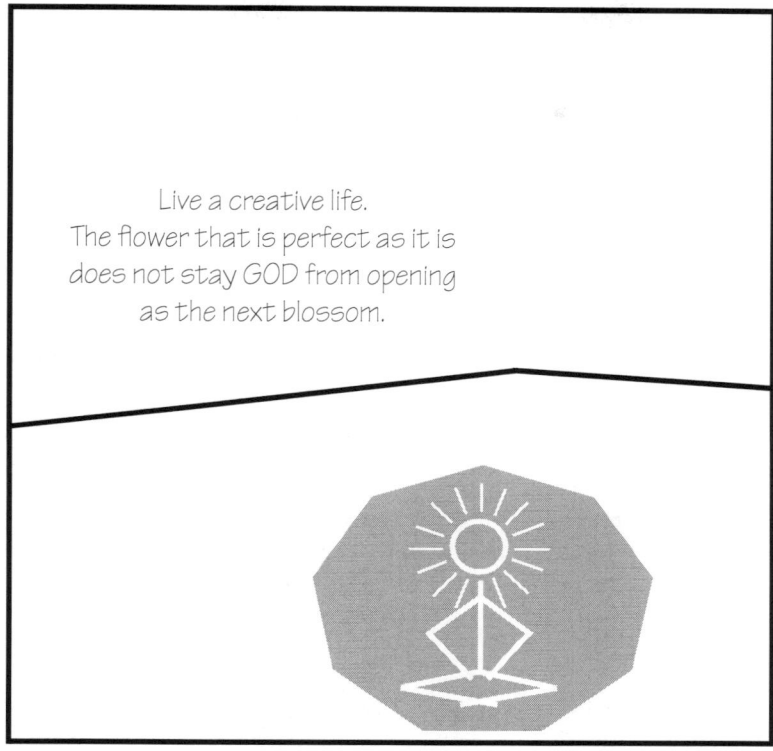

Live a creative life.
The flower that is perfect as it is
does not stay GOD from opening
as the next blossom.

Creativity.

Awakening frees you from being a slave to form.

Living awake allows you to play joyfully with form
without attachment or expectation.

Maybe GOD dreamed of you as a painter
so she could paint.
Maybe GOD dreamed of you as a poet
so he could write.
Maybe God dreamed of you as a dancer
so she could dance.
Maybe...

Musings

 Out of stillness, right action arises

Another myth of pure awareness is that on the other side of enlightenment, there will be nothing to be done and no one left to do it. This idea comes from the sloppily constructed notion that since the world is perfect as it is and there is no separate doer left, there must be nothing to be done. So we will all sit around on cushions all day contemplating perfection. Each of these elements is true enough, but the conclusion is still mistaken.

The world is perfect as it is. The pain and the pleasure, the sudden and tragic death of one baby or millions of people, the bliss of love, the joy of a new birth, a rape, a caress, a murder, a kiss, the sunset and the tsunami are all perfect as they are. How could they not be. They are all GOD.

Much of what we experience as "doing" in our lives is compulsive and driven by the desire to fill the emptiness that the illusion of separation creates inside of us. It is that "doer" that dies, but enlightenment is not meant to incapacitate us.

If this is all GOD's plan, then there is nothing we need to do. But, seen another way, if this is GOD's plan, then there is nothing that needs to be done except what GOD wants us to do and since we cannot know what GOD wants us to do or not do, why assume GOD wants us to do nothing?

As GOD's perfect world unfolds, we will still experience feelings and thoughts, and sometimes those feelings and thoughts will lead to actions that need doing. Compassion will ground those actions in the truth of oneness. Curiosity will ensure that we see clearly what is before us and that we don't come to identify with the actions we take. Creativity will keep our actions spontaneous. Stillness and presence will ensure that as GOD's actors, we improvise with clarity and without hesitation.

*Spend a lot of time sitting in stillness until
the action that must be taken arises.
Then act without fear or hesitation.*

Right Action.

Compassion is not passive.

Compassion is not without passion.

The death of the doer is not the end of doing.

It is the end of mindless, compulsive doing
that distracts us from the suffering
we create when we misunderstand
the nature of reality.

Musings

 Humor arises

An identity is an illusion, but it is a heavy illusion. We actually have multiple identities that we seem to need to have ready to whip out at any moment for different situations. Carrying those identities around with us all the time has a dampening effect. On the other side of enlightenment, the heaviness of self is lifted. Another word for the heaviness of self is seriousness or self-importance. When seriousness (which is a condition, as opposed to simply responding to what arises in a serious manner) is lifted, what is liberated is a sense of humor.

When humor arises on the other side of enlightenment, it is the humor of seeing our own folly and foolishness. It is GOD's sense of humor. It is the laughter of the child discovering something surprising for the first time.

I will confess to having a litmus test for spiritual teachers and spiritual paths: how much do they laugh and how much is laughter encouraged? Of course, there is a humor of scorn, derision, and humiliation. This is the laughter and humor of separation—what makes me and mine better than you and yours. But what I am talking about is the laughter of recognition—the humor of the comic who points out the foolishness of the belief to which we are clinging and upon which we are building a separate identity.

Can you laugh with patience when you catch yourself clinging to the way something "should" be? Can you laugh with recognition when you discover a persistent little "me" that somehow did not get the nondual change-of-management memo? Can you laugh with wonder at how simple it actually all is once attention returns to your "oceanness" as opposed to your "waveness?"

And, finally, practice laughing.

Humor.

None of us gets it right all the time.

When being compassionate is exhausting,
and curiosity in the face of the mystery
has revealed more than we wanted to know,
and our impermanent creative projects are a bit
more impermanent than we had hoped for,
and we realize that with the best of intentions
our spiritual actions had consequences
we did not anticipate,
all we can really do is laugh.

MUSINGS:

 Fear waves or love waves

We arise out of the ocean that is consciousness and take these beautiful wave forms for periods of time and then dissolve back into the ocean. It actually takes energy to hold the form of a wave and in childhood and youth we generally cultivate our wave-ness and sacrifice our ocean-ness. We see other waves around us. Some waves are bigger and some are smaller. Some threaten to engulf us and some we can engulf. In taking and holding these wave forms, we forget that we are all made of ocean. Our wave forms become our identities.

So it seems to me that we can be waves in one of two ways— in fear or in love. In fear, we forget our true nature as ocean (love). We become preoccupied with remaining as the wave- forms with which we identify. We close down in the face of other waves. We see them as threats and challenges. We are not less ocean (love) because of our fear, but we do add suffering to the game of being a wave. We fear poverty, illness, aging, and death, because all we know is either wave or no-wave.

As love, we simply remember our nature as ocean. We under- stand that this is all temporary. We don't need to experience death in order to reconstitute as a new wave-form. We realize that, in reality, we are always becoming a new wave. We do not fear or judge other waves, but rather recognize our ocean-ness in them. We may still choose to avoid other waves that would engulf or overwhelm us, but not out of fear. Rather we would simply be playing the game of being a wave, with bliss and abandon and detachment.

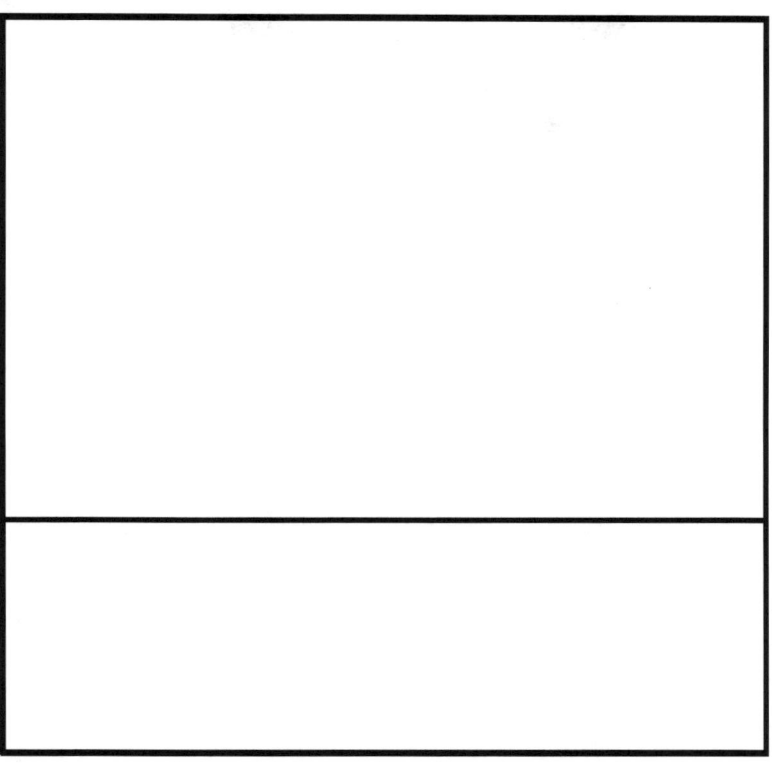

May you get to the point
where you are no longer
looking for yourself
in what arises.

May you actually awaken to the truth
that you are the one
that was before you were born
and will be after you are dead.

Chapter Nine
Saying No To GOD

If GOD is everywhere and everything, if he is constantly inviting us to wake up and remember the
truth of our oneness, why do we constantly say no
to GOD.

Or, on a more personal level,
why have I consistently said no to GOD.

CONFESSION

I have been afraid.

During much of the 1990's I studied various forms of energetic healing with a variety of teachers. I was very successful in classroom settings, which felt great to my sense of identity, but was ultimately very safe, because those people wanted to support me as a healer and wanted to feel an effect and wanted to believe.

When I had my first opportunity to work with someone who did not have an interest in my being successful, the success I experienced and the relief of symptoms she felt was huge for me. Huge and terrifying. I stumbled through a period of my life working with people in hospitals and with serious and life-threatening conditions. I had nurses comment on how even the vital signs of patients in comas improved when I worked on them.

I should have been ecstatic. This is what I had always thought I wanted to do or be. GOD was giving me every bit of confirmation my skeptical mind could handle and all I could think of to say to GOD was "No thanks!"

I was afraid of what it would mean to "my" life and "my" plans, and "my" desire to direct "my" life. So much "me," so little time. Like most people, I was not miserable. I just wanted to increase the level and consistency of my happiness. I have always been blessed (or cursed) with the capacity to make the best of the situations in which I found myself. I was not suffering on the surface. I wasn't openly angry or clearly in despair, but I was afraid. I was afraid that there might not be a GOD and, at the same time, afraid that GOD might take too active an interest in my personal life. I was afraid of what would happen if I let go of my sense of control and started to play GOD's game.

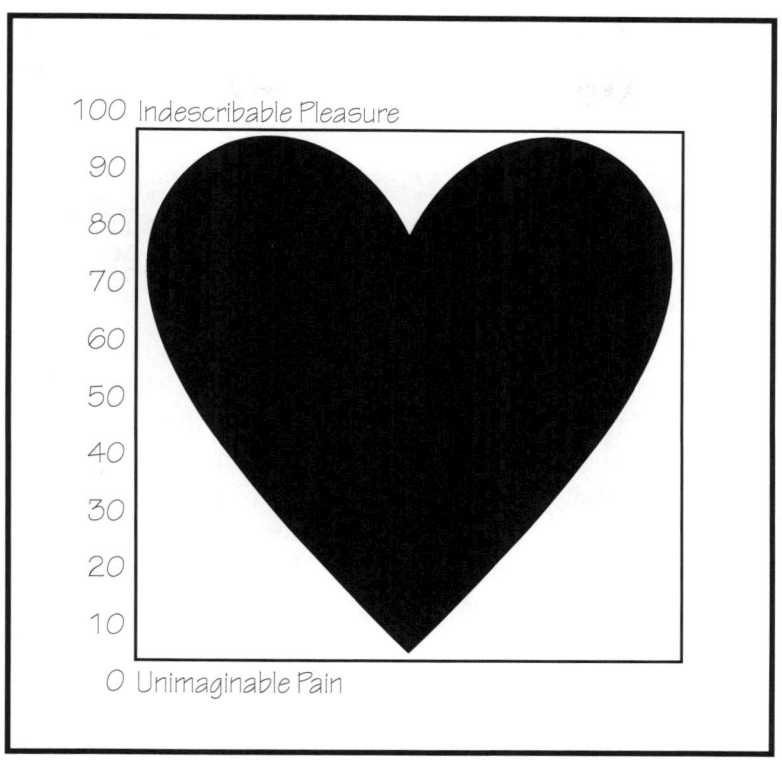

Imagine for a moment that the full range
of what a wide awake human might be capable of
experiencing in this incarnation
could be described on a scale of 0 to 100.

Let's allow 0 to represent the most unimaginable
pain (physical or emotional) and 100 to represent
the most indescribable pleasure.

These experiences are merely
the ways GOD has of vibrating.

At that point in my life, I was also seduced by a new relationship into thinking that I really had found that elusive external source of happiness. I did not want enlightenment. The death of my ego did not sound like a good thing, especially to my ego. I just wanted to know how to play the game better.

I continued to write and teach and counsel people and I was good at it. I was good at helping people play the game better, but underneath it all I was afraid.

I was afraid of the truth of oneness I had tasted in Ayahuasca ceremonies with a Peruvian shaman. I was afraid of the heart opening lack of separation I touched in all night Veladas (Mazatec sacred mushroom ceremonies) in Juatla, Mexico. I was afraid of those moments of absolute dissolution in sexual intimacy with my beloved, as all boundaries between two people seemed to evaporate. I was afraid of the true emptiness of the void that I touched in my deepest meditation. I was afraid of not looking and afraid of finding what I was looking for. I was afraid of the mask of identity I wore and afraid that everyone would find out that I was wearing a mask.

In a meditation with Master Charles Cannon at the Synchronicity ashram in the mountains of Virginia I heard the voice of my fear more clearly than I ever had. I realized that I had spent most of my adult life preparing for a test that I was certain I was going to fail. I was not proud of this. I was not pleased by this revelation. I realized that just as I had said no to GOD moving through me as a healer, I was continuing to say no to the recognition of the truth of who I was—who we all are—as if by continuing to say no, I could postpone the final exam just a little while longer.

I said no to GOD—we say no to GOD—out of fear. We want GOD, we ache for that union, and yet we say no and no and no again.

As I wrote in the introduction, I was not looking for enlight-

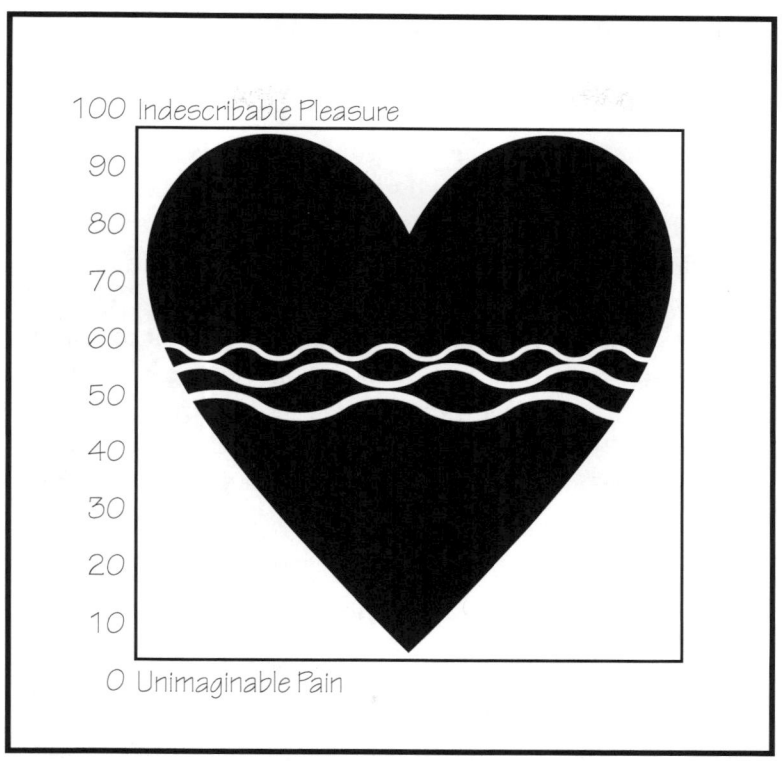

GOD's vibrations are not
"my" feelings or "my" emotions.
They are merely the temperature of the water.

But in the dream of separation
the isolated wave I believe myself to be
feels hot or cold
and "I" lay claim to that temperature.
I suffer that temperature as mine and mine alone.
I look around for causes for the things I am feeling.
Causes are reasons and reasons create meaning
and meaning reinforces my sense
of uniqueness and separation.

enment. I was not aiming for it, studying it, or aspiring to it. When I had the experience that would become the genesis for this book, I did not even tell anyone about it.

The concepts and ideas behind pure awareness and nonduality often feel like GOD's shell game. Wherever you think the pea is, it isn't. Most of us just want to play the game better. We believe in self-help and transformation. We don't want to question the illusion. We don't want to know that the wizard is just an old man behind a curtain. We don't want to risk everything to bring back the witch's broom only to be told that we had all the heart and knowledge and courage we could ever need all along. But if we don't pull back the curtain, if we don't develop an appetite for the truth, we will never get home.

As a very young child, some of my earliest memories were my fantasies that I could help people who seemed sad or hurt, whether I knew them or not. In some respects, I've lived that life, but ultimately, really helping people has to be about waking up from the illusion of separation. Everything else is decoration, new paint and wallpaper over a mildew-laden suffering that will eventually eat through that bright facade.

I understand that this is not for everyone. It isn't easy. It's hard and it's radical and it requires us to face our fears and move counter to the beliefs of family and society. It's not comfortable and it's not convenient and unless we stop anesthetizing ourselves to how much we are suffering, we will never want the truth badly enough to make that leap.

Claiming enlightenment always sounds slightly pretentious, but I have no doubt that the more people who are able to wake up to the radical truth of the oneness of all beings and all forms, the better it will be for everyone. Nondual or pure awareness is not an abstract philosophy.

I said at the beginning of the book that enlightenment is not a self-help program and yet, in some ways it is the ultimate

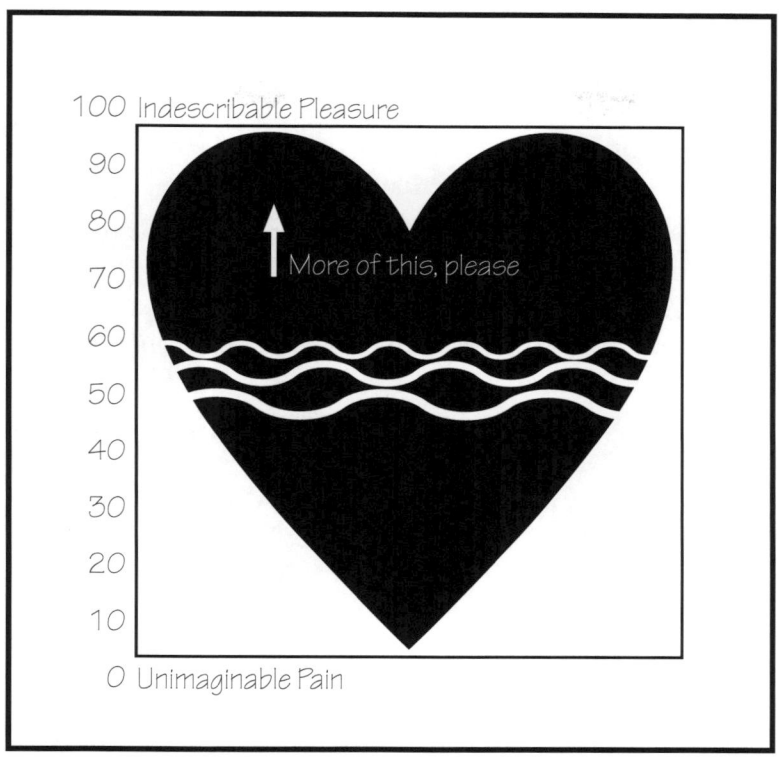

As a separate wave in GOD's dream
I imagine that I can move myself
over warmer or cooler water.
I believe I can control my experience
of GOD's vibration.

When I believe it's working
I'm happy.
When I believe it isn't working
I'm suffering.

Of course it's all a fantasy,
but then, I'm dreaming, what do I really know?

self-help program.

It is the belief in the separate self, the failure to open as love and engaged compassion, that keeps us in suffering. We cling to the leaking life rafts of our separate and isolated identities and ignore the outstretched hand of GOD.

There is not a problem that we face from birth to death in this incarnation that would not be better met with the truth of our divine unity. As the Vedantic sages wrote, and as the Buddha said, we suffer and we create suffering because we misperceive the true nature of the world. All the pain we inflict upon others and upon ourselves is caused by the lack we feel and our reckless desire to feel whole.

Jeff Foster writes in "An Extraordinary Absence: Liberation in the Midst of a Very Ordinary Life," *At the root of all the seeking of a lifetime is a sense of not being whole. Of being incomplete. Fragmented. Lost. Alienated. Homesick.*

We create such suffering in our illusion of separation, commit such crimes from behind the walls of our well-defended identities, make such poor choices by always seeking what is beyond the here and the now, and wound so deeply from our longing to return to a unity that we deny and refuse. The only way home is through the ultimate truth of our oneness—waking up.

Behind and beneath all my fear is the perfect empty projection screen (and I promise that this is the last time that I will use the movie projection metaphor in this book). My thoughts and feelings and recollections and fantasies are like movies that play across that screen. For awhile that movie is a romantic comedy and that is my life. Then a horror film is playing and that is my life. Next is a drama, then an action picture and then a mystery. I use each movie (all the elements and emotions that are evoked) to construct my identity. They become who I am and how I see myself.

I forget that I am not those movies and they are not me. They

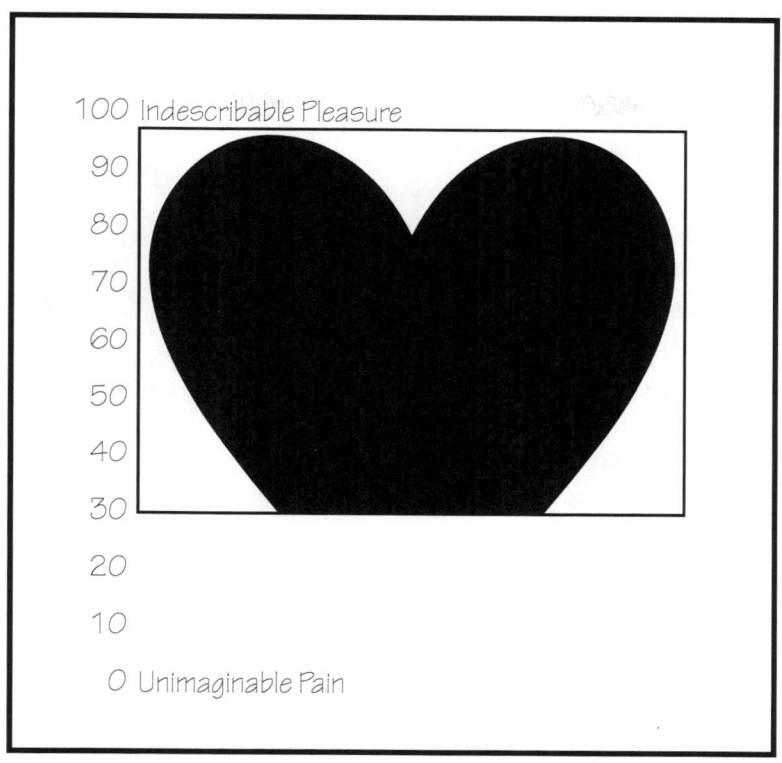

I love "my" pleasure,
and in my dream, I say
that I want love and joy without limits.
But I also come to fear my pain
so I protect myself
in order to limit my exposure to pain.

I do this by isolating my self even more,
by shutting down my capacity to feel pain,
by creating a window of exposure to life that says
I want no pain worse than 30.

The number is arbitrary, but you get the point.

are simply what is playing across the screen inside me. When I meditate, when I penetrate with deep questions, I know this to be true.

There is a scene in the film "Scrooged" where Bill Murray's character is responding to a comment from the ghost of Christmas past that he had spent his life sitting in front of a TV screen. He argues that he remembers doing significant things, but everything he remembers is actually an episode from a TV program he watched as a child.

Beginning to wake up is what this feels like. We realize that the selves we are so certain we are don't really exist. They are thought-movies that we have been clinging to. They are images that once played across our internal screens and which we unconsciously coopted to create identities, and now we find ourselves defending them without question.

When someone or some experience reminds us that we are actually the screen and not the movies we've had projected upon us, it triggers fear—which often expresses as anger. When anger or fear arises, it is a good indication that an unconscious boundary or edge is being hit. All fear arises from the perception that we are separate and finite beings. If this is true, then we can die or lose those things that make us who we believe we are. They can be taken away from us by other separate selves. The world is not a safe place and we are not safe in it. We cannot relax for a moment.

Fear is the wolf at the door. It is that thing that keeps us protected and defended and apart from everything we most long to embrace. Fear, in itself, is simply a reaction. Sometimes it is an appropriate human reaction. It helps us survive and can help us make prudent choices. The problem is when we convert the experience of fear arising into permanent or near permanent state. When fear moves from being something we experience to being something we are, we cannot help but say no to GOD.

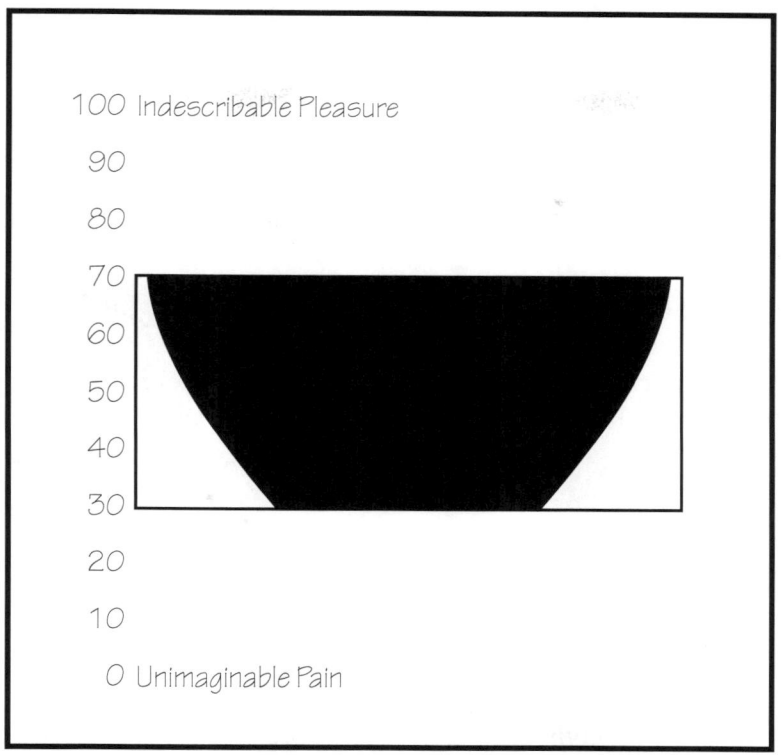

100 Indescribable Pleasure
90
80
70
60
50
40
30
20
10
0 Unimaginable Pain

But, in my self-imposed isolation,
the upper threshold for how much
love and joy I can feel, is limited as well.

I cannot close my heart to pain
without closing my heart to joy.

The more I believe myself to be
separate and isolated and unique and alone,
the more I create a small window of experience
that is acceptable, while denying my heart
the full spectrum of experience (GOD's vibration)
and creating suffering.

We say no to GOD when we come to believe that the frightening movies of victims that have played across our screens are who we are.

On the other side of enlightenment, when the wolf growls at the door, we open it. We let the wolf in. We give the wolf space. We turn the lights on. We meet our fears. We come to know our fears.

Listening to the voice of fear—simply acknowledging it—is not the same thing as acting from our fears. We will not let the wolf drag us back into the dark forest, but neither will we barricade our doors and live in fear of what might be.

I can find and hold the paradox that at the same time it feels as if there is some urgency to more and more separate selves waking up to the truth of who and what we are <u>and</u> that it feels as if there is absolutely nothing that needs to be done. Here and now is an infinite space-time.

In the end it comes down to this. Pure awareness already exists in each of us. It exists in the space between the thoughts and in the thoughts themselves.

We live in the light, but we have our eyes closed. Enlightenment is as easy as opening our eyes.

Liberation is not a struggle. We built the prison. We made the chains. We have the key. We have always had the key.

And even though we are asleep, GOD is nudging us to wake up.

Waking up from the dream is a huge risk.
GOD's vibrations don't cease.
They continue to rise and fall,
the temperature shifts.
But there is no "me" there
to lay claim to those emotions.

As an awakened wave, as pure awareness,
vibration arises and tears come
or laughter.
But they find nothing to cling to
and there is no "I" to cling to them.

INVITATION

We say no to GOD because we are afraid.

A single drop of illuminating nectar falls
through infinite space and time,
wanting to splash across your tongue
in one bright and blazing taste of pure awareness.

Your eyes are sealed shut,
heart closed,
fists clenched,
lips pursed in fear,
and yet,
you want that taste.

This will change everything,
and yet,
you want that taste.

This is your death and your dissolution,
and yet,
you want that taste.

This is the annihilation of tomorrow
and the extinction of yesterday,
and yet,
you want that taste.

Let's stand together,
eyes wide open, tongues outstretched,
with everything to lose and everything to gain,
and let's say yes to GOD.

And so love begins.

Remember,
this line is GOD,
this line is LOVE,
this line is CONSCIOUSNESS.

It is pure potential.
There is nothing that is not this line.
There is no form this line cannot draw.
We are all drawn of the same line.
Everything is drawn of the same line.

Something and nothing.

Epilogue
Strange Attractors

I have spent a good part of my life studying and
practicing shamanism and working with dreams.
On the surface, this is an odd pedigree for someone
teaching and writing about nonduality. The more
common path is through some tradition of eastern
spirituality or exposure to a particular guru.
I get this question often enough that I think it is
worth addressing:
How does a shaman come to nonduality?

I should begin by saying that my conception and practice of shamanism has evolved over time and is not the commonly accepted view in the neo-shamanic community. This evolution is something I began to describe in my book *Stone Age Wisdom: The Healing Principles of Shamanism* and has continued to grow. It is not the stereotypical view of shamanism. It is neither a cultural appropriation nor does it require a regression to some pre-rational stage of awareness in order to accept and practice. I have taken to referring to it as an integral shamanism to distinguish it from what is commonly practiced but in so doing, I mean no disrespect to traditional shamans or neo-shamanic practitioners.

In the book "*The Master Game*" Robert DeRopp writes: "What people really need and demand from life is not wealth, comfort, or esteem, but games worth playing." He goes on to elaborate that: "We can divide life into object games and meta games. Object games can be thought of as games for the attainment of material things, primarily money and the objects which money can buy. Meta games are played for intangibles such as knowledge or the salvation of the soul."

While I think this conception is useful, I would argue that what we are really playing are state games. We want to attain some state of consciousness like peace, happiness, contentment, fulfillment, wholeness, health or love. We play object games because we mistakenly come to associate a desired state with the acquisition of certain material conditions, relationships, or situations.

The ultimate state game is the awakening game.

Whether you are an anonymous tribal shaman or one of the founders of the world's great religions, the underlying premise of the meta game of spirituality is that we are asleep and living in a dream world. The evolution of the awakening game over time has taken us from the shamans who were the early pioneers of transcendence and consciousness to the Buddhas and beyond.

Shamans were probably the first explorers of consciousness, so it makes sense that at least some shamans must have been the first to stumble upon the truth that consciousness is everything or everything is consciousness. Of course how that truth was understood or communicated depended upon the cultural stage of evolution of that particular shaman.

Shamans, to the level they were allowed by their cultures, developed tools and techniques for awakening to the true nature of reality and exploring consciousness itself. Of course those techniques were subject to a cultural overlay that was usually animist or based in nature and ancestor worship, but the techniques themselves were profound and would evolve into the meditative and contemplative practices that are at the core of the world's great religions.

Because shamanism evolved among nomadic peoples for whom physical survival was of paramount importance, it tended to have very practical applications such as locating prey (elk, buffalo, whales), healing illness and injury, and caring for the emotional psyche of the tribe. Ultimately this led to shamanism developing powerful techniques and practices for attending to the unseen dimensions of the waking world or the world of form, but stopped short of the idea that all people might awaken from the dream.

Ken Wilber writes about three great states of consciousness that seem to appear in both the great religious traditions and in our own day-to-day experience. These states are the gross (physical), subtle (dreaming), and causal (formless emptiness). In the "state game" that has been my life, I was drawn by a deep fascination with dreams and dreaming states and the desire to do healing work. It led me to explore shamanic practices (the spirituality of the gross physical world—mother nature—Gaia—the circle of life and other third-person forms of meeting the face of God). Shamanic techniques like enhanced awareness of energetic flow, focused attention, and sensitivity to the patterns that lie beneath the manifestation of form in the material realm do help one play the game more artfully and with more effectiveness. As my path progressed, however, I was also drawn to the idea of not just playing the game better, but of waking up from the game itself. Because, in the end, playing the game better, even mastering the game, only takes one so far.

For me shamanism is first and foremost the exploration of consciousness. It is a sensitivity to the way energy, as a kind of template for arising form, moves and flows. Borrowing terminology from physics, shamanism is a sensitivity to or fascination with strange attractors—what creates patterns out of chaos. All the specific techniques that seem so exotic and strange are really just a cultural overlay for developing, enhancing, and refining a specific set of skills and techniques for working at the intersection of form and formlessness.

Because of a deep desire to serve and help others, I have spent a lot of time counseling and coaching in ways that sometimes look shamanic and other times look like satsang and still other times look like an exchange between a therapist and client. What I have found is that in my own life I have little patience for further empowering my illusions, but when it comes to helping others, the principles and techniques of shamanism and dreamwork have value. This is why I think it is relevant to blend an integral form of shamanism with dreamwork and nonduality. In the gross realm, shamanism can be highly useful. In the subtle realm, dreams give us guidance and clarity in the dialog between the dream and the dreamer. Nonduality places all of this in perspective.

The physics of Einstein and Newton describes the visible world in elegant and predictable ways. But when we approach the subatomic level the math that predicts phenomenon so consistently collapses and we need a new math, a new physics—quantum mechanics. The search that drives cutting-edge physics today, however, is for a unifying theory that brings together the macro and the micro realms.

Science and technology describe the physical world with a high degree of predictability, but there are some realms in which science seems to break down. Shamanism is, for me, like quantum physics. When you strip away the layers of cultural decoration, the history of animism, and the cosmology of tribal deities and forces, shamanism does a good job of describing and even intervening locally in an energetic phenomena that we do not readily perceive or fully understand.

Nonduality, for me, is a search for a unified field theory.

Of course I also know that all of this—from shamanism through dreamwork and including everything I might say about nonduality—is just a story that I am telling myself.

Awhile back the radio program *"All Things Considered"* from National Public Radio did a series of pieces from different experts with different perspectives about what makes us human or what seems to set us apart from other animals. One of my favorites was an anthropologist who said that we may be human because we tell stories.

I personally have an on-again-off-again love affair with stories. I always have. I love stories <u>and</u> I struggle to remember and to remind others that they are, in the end, just stories. They are one of the unique ways we communicate thoughts, feelings, and sensations and try to make sense of what is often such a mystery.

Most of the time, when you ask a question that begins with why, whether you know it or not, you are inviting someone to tell you a story. Don't be upset when they give you a story. It is really the best that anyone can do in the face of "why?"

A friend of mine, Susan, asked the question: Why do some people seem to affect us so much and others not at all? There is, of course no real answer to this question. There are only stories, but one of the stories that seems to address this question is that we incarnate in this realm with "soul contracts" with other souls that also incarnate here. Those people that affect us in powerful and meaningful ways are those with whom we have an agreement to help us work out or work through certain issues in this realm.

There are two variations of the soul contract idea. One is that we have these soul contracts to work through issues that in some way evolve our spirits from lifetime to lifetime. Another is that working through these issues has nothing to do with an evolutionary movement because when we die we return to that undifferentiated consciousness from whose perspective there is no need to evolve. That "story" holds that we have soul contracts simply so that the GOD/LOVE/Consciousness that we all are can have experiences in differentiated form: in essence, so that we can play the great game without knowing the ending.

There are, of course, subtle variations of the soul contract story that attempt to integrate both of these perspectives. I happen to like this story, whether it is true or not, because it shifts my relationship to people I do not like and I think any story that helps me move in the direction of tolerance and compassion and forgiveness is a good thing.

While working on this book, I had this dream:

I'm with my wife, Kelly, in a big, old, marble-columned building where there is a party going on. It is a costume party and to get in, everyone has to have a costume and a mask. One of the "rules" of the party is that your costume and your mask determine how you interact with other costumes and masks. I am in some kind of swashbuckling costume with a sword and a mask and a big hat. Kelly is in a long, low-cut dress from the same period so our relationship seems predetermined. We are supposed to flirt and fight but end up together. It is obvious what my relationship to some people is supposed to be (attractive women, noble comrades-in-arms, wise mentors, sidekicks, villains, archenemies, tyrants, etc.), but some of them are more confusing. When I meet people I am not supposed to like (because of their costumes and mine), I find that I actually don't like them. They fulfill my expectations of being unlikable. The upshot is that some people I like and some people I don't and these people have a strong affect upon me. There are, however, a lot of people that I don't seem to feel strongly about one way or the other.

As the party progresses, I am dancing/flirting with a woman who I am sure is not Kelly, but it turns out that behind her mask, she is Kelly. I become aware that every woman that I am attracted to is actually Kelly. Then I begin to notice that the men look familiar. We begin nodding at each other, smiling and winking in secret recognition. I realize that they are all me—even the ones that I am not supposed to like (because of their costumes and masks).

Eventually, I begin to realize that even the women I am attracted to (the Kellys) are also me. This is the most amazing feeling. At first it is strange. They all do not look like me. They still look very different and they still have their masks and costumes, but I know they are really me. I know that this probably sounds very narcissistic, but it didn't make me feel important or like I was the center of anything. On the contrary, my sense of self seemed much more diffuse. It was also really relaxing, because I no longer had anything to fear or to hide, because they were me. There was nothing and nowhere to hide anyway.

The odd thing is that in the dream we still played the game of interacting as lovers or friends or students or teachers or enemies, but we did it playfully and without any real attachment to that relationship being right or true or anything other than a momentary exchange. I could still feel myself gravitating toward strong attraction (like) or revulsion (dislike).

So my dream doesn't really answer Susan's "why" question, except in the sense that one reason that people affect us so profoundly is that it may be us (as GOD) affecting us (as GOD) and that when we meet someone to whom we are attracted or repulsed, it is really a kind of recognition process.

We recognize things we like about ourselves in others and things we dislike about ourselves in others and that is what is affecting us. When people don't affect us, perhaps it is that we are not recognizing ourselves in them.

This, of course, begs the question, would enlightenment or awakening actually mean that we were more affected or affected by more people (increasing the amount of feeling we have) because we recognize ourselves in more people? Or, would it mean that we were less affected because the highs and lows were neutralized by recognizing ourselves in everyone and we no longer took being affected so seriously?

Again, these are just stories, regardless of how truthful or convincing they may sound. As an author and teacher it is my job to sound authoritative, but I am more convinced than ever that while "good stories" are useful in helping us master the game and even in getting us *to* the threshold of awakening, "*no stories*" are the words inscribed on the threshold of awakening itself.

So in my case, the answer to the question of how a shaman ends up at nonduality can be summed up in the admission that I have spent my life following the path of ever better and larger stories into the realm of no stories at all.

> *Hell is a story about life as a series of random and meaningless events, some painful, some joyful, but ultimately going nowhere and signifying nothing.*

> *Heaven is a story of life as an intricately choreographed dance of relationships and experiences designed to refine our capacity for consciousness, compassion, and creativity.*

> *Enlightenment is a life without story—simply a conscious, compassionate, and creative response to what arises moment-to-moment.*

Appendix

Learning More About Nothing

This book was written to communicate some of the basic concepts of nonduality and pure awareness, through an admittedly flawed filter. If you didn't already know this, there are far more eloquent guides to the territory of nonduality with a great variety of perspectives. If you want to learn more about enlightenment and pure awareness, these are some of the most interesting writers and teachers I've come across. While they are not all, strictly speaking, "nondual teachers," they are useful. Some of these people are beloved and some are loathed, but they all have interesting things to say (apparently, awakening or aspiring to pure awareness doesn't interfere with our capacity or desire to judge others).

Enjoy the adventure.

Chris Hebard: *www.stillnessspeaks.com*
Start here! This Website is the best video clip resource there is for those using direct inquiry as a path to enlightenment. You can see great video clips of some of the teachers and authors, I've listed below.

Adyashanti: *www.adyashanti.org*
Spontaneous awakening in accessible language.

Master Charles Cannon: *www.synchronicity.org*
High tech meditation and nondual teaching from a mystical scientist.

Andrew Cohen: *www.andrewcohen.org*
Spiritual teacher, author, and publisher of EnlightenNext magazine.

David Deida: *www.deida.info*
The yoga of intimate relationship and the author of "Instant Enlightenment."

Jeff Foster: *www.lifewithoutacentre.com*
Proof that youth (or awakening) is not always wasted on the young. I wish I knew what he knows when I was his age.

Gangaji: *www.gangaji.org*
Just stop looking.

Greg Goode: *www.heartofnow.com*
Nondual teacher and author of "Standing as Awareness."

Paul Hedderman: *www.zenbitchslap.com*
If you like the rough stuff. Edgy, "get over yourself" nonduality.

Chuck Hillig: *www.chuckhillig.com*
The only other person I know who is illustrating enlightenment.

Byron Katie: *www.thework.com*
What happens when you apply nondual awareness to the problems that most concern people.

Loch Kelly: *www.lochkelly.org*
Nondual teacher with a gift for pointing you towards pure awareness.

Scott Kiloby: *www.kiloby.com*
First there is a concept then there is no concept, then there is.

Peter Kingsley: *www.peterkingsley.org*
Nonduality in the pre-Socratic Western tradition.

Francis Lucille: *www.francislucille.com*
Why does Advaita always sound better with a French accent?

Dennis Merzel: *www.bigmind.org*
Big Mind—Big Heart.

Candice O'Denver: *www.greatfreedom.org*
Short moments of clarity repeated many times.

Daniel Odier: *www.danielodier.com*
Spiritual teacher and author of "Desire, the Tantric Path to Awakening."

Rupert Spira: *www.rupertspira.com*
Beautiful words. Beautiful objects.

James Swartz: *www.shiningworld.com*
Getting serious about Vedanta.

Robert Thurman: *www.ted.com/talks/bob_thurman_says_ we_can_be_buddhas.html*
The most fun you can have learning about Buddhism.

Eckhart Tolle: *www.eckharttolle.com*
While it seems fashionable to dismiss Eckhart these days, more people have been exposed to the ideas of nonduality through his work than from any other teacher. That should probably count for something.

Ken Wilber: *www.kenwilber.com/home/landing/index.html*
The cartographer of consciousness.

Stephen Wolinsky: *www.stephenhwolinskyphdlibrary.com*
The Western voice of Nisargadatta Maharaj.

BLISS DREAMING

Tom does talks and lectures on nonduality,
specifically with practical applications
for living a householder's path
with greater love and deeper consciousness.

He does individual energetic counseling for clarity,
As well as dreamwork and coaching
from a nondual perspective.
For more information about Tom
you can visit his website at
www.blissdreaming.com
or contact him at
tom@blissdreaming.com

Made in the USA
Charleston, SC
15 March 2011